100 Things to Know and Debate Before You Vote

HINDOL SENGUPTA is Senior Editor at the Indian edition of *Fortune* magazine. He is the author of three previous books including *The Liberals*. He is founder of the not for profit open government platform, the Whypoll Trust, and the Paperweight design project. He was voted by the global ideas platform IdeaMensch on its 2012 list of 32 Entrepreneurs Who Make The World A Better Place.

100 Things to Know and Debate Before You Vote

HINDOL SENGUPTA

HarperCollins *Publishers* India

First published in India by
HarperCollins *Publishers* in 2014

Building 10, Tower A, 4th Floor, DLF Cyber City, Phase II,
Gurugram Haryana – 122002, India
www.harpercollins.co.in

2 4 6 8 10 9 7 5 3

P-ISBN: 978-93-5136-221-0
E-ISBN: 978-93-5136-222-7

Typeset in 10.5/14 Minion
by Jojy Philip, New Delhi 110 015

Printed and bound at
MicroPrints India, New Delhi

To my parents, who always said,
'We are simple, middle class people.
All this politics is dirty and violent. It is not for us.'

"The world is a dangerous place to live, not because of the people who are evil, but because of the people who don't do anything about it."

— Albert Einstein

1. Citizen, Unrest

This, around us, is a strange disquiet. Have you felt it? For more than a year, or was it two, the breathless air has smelt of something about to happen, and on the streets, on blinking screens, the velocity of all that we have wanted to say for so long a time, and now, all at once, it is coming out, stammering, stuttering, in a tripping babble.

It is not the past we crave, it is not nostalgia, which is so often an affectation of the elite, but we are those who mourn the future that never quite arrived, and for a while now, has seemed irretrievably delayed.

There is an election coming, its approach complete with the slowness of a storm. But we in India, so proud and petulant about our democracy, are used to elections here and there in our multicoloured ways every season. What, then, is different?

Sometimes in the varied histories of old, old countries, there comes that time when the gossip in the capital begins to smell like rotten food, or fish. It is the smell of the shedding of skin, it is the smell of change.

We are those whose per capita hope refuses to live up to its initial market potential

Newspapers that are dying (because people, afraid of missing a single update, are absorbed in hash-tags and home-pages) claim all revolutions, even those that remain only in the mind, smell like this.

When you step out, in a few weeks, to colour your nail black, and cast—do they call it cast because it is as whimsical, and equally numbing, as fishing—your vote, what will you be thinking? Will you be thinking of what you could have been, even become, and have? Or, haven't? Will you think of battles, hard fought and won, even lost? Will you think of the promise of democracy—that in the journey you shall find yourself?

This will be an election which will be what elections rarely are—not just about what the grand future idea of India will be but also about what the idea of who you will be in the future; your vote will be your private crystal ball, the poll will be a palm reading.

If you are going to vote in a few weeks, you would have felt this fragility, this sense of collective mortality that makes democrats of citizens. There is a sense that this is the end. But an end of what exactly? And what, precisely, follows?

We have some of the worst roads in the world, our air is poisoned, we drink polluted water, in disease we are consistent world beaters but not so in Olympian sport, or efficiency, or honesty. In almost every global parameter of development, we are at the bottom. Tens of thousands die of ill-treatment every year, millions more are impoverished by the cost of healthcare. There is fraud everywhere, even at our National Library. But what we get for national debate—even before a vital election—is name calling, abuse and derision. Our leaders are so accustomed to thinking of us in the mute that they laugh that it is enough to give us some entertainment, some ring fighting, for if the people can watch the lions fight, why should they ask for governance?

In reality, an election is not so much about answers—though some answers it certainly provides—but also questions, introspections into who we are and what we should have been or perhaps failed to become. All elections, then, are exercises in sociological séances where the spirits of the past cast long shadows on our present, even future. Does that not sound a bit like this trumpeted national battle between Rahul Gandhi of the Congress Party and Narendra Modi of the Bharatiya Janata Party? But they are not the only ones lumbering towards glory. Every state, every village has gamblers and game-changers. The comprehensive bet of the *aam aadmi* is almost too awkward to contemplate. But bet we shall—all of us and the 149 million who will be us for the first time—the choice is upon us and this book is about one hundred things you might want to think about before you cast that vote. Which way will you toss?

There has been for the last two decades a creeping belief, a steady rise in per capita hope that things were incrementally, sometimes assiduously, getting better. After all, if you go by the estimates of the Planning Commission, just between 2004 and 2010, poverty levels in India declined by nearly 10 per cent from 37.2 per cent to 29.8 per cent, and officially we have only 269.3 million people who are defined as poor. Of these, 216.5 million (80 per cent), live in rural India.

But the latest initiative of the Indian government is to provide food at very low costs to around 67 per cent of our more than 1.2 billion people. This then raises the question—why is it that 67 per cent of Indians need assistance for something as basic as fighting hunger if millions are being pulled out of poverty?

This is the point where our per capita hope falters. There is that feeling, which you often get as an Indian citizen, that someone somewhere is not telling you the truth. Something is going wrong.

You will realise during the course of this book that indeed something is.

With terrifying standards in everything from personal hygiene to financial probity, Indian democracy is gravely imperilled. But is that the debate you hear? Is that what resonates across campaign speeches? Assailed by the question of who are we to vote for, we are forgetting the other vital question—what are we to vote for?

We argue in this book that we ought to vote on issues most critical to us, reflecting our national failures and successes, and for people who deliver those to us. With every issue raised in this book, all one hundred of them, there are questions in *sotto voce*—who do you think can solve this? Should you not vote for the person you think can solve this?

As a journalist I have often felt that I live in a country where no stakeholder, to use that public policy term, really understands or wants to understand one another. The NGO folks are disdainful about the corporate types, CEOs laugh at *jhola-wallah* do-gooders, public policy gurus pour scorn on politicians and *netas* sometimes seem to be laughing at us all. Yet, India needs, more than ever perhaps, everyone to really try and understand each other and work with one another. It is now clear that neither growth, nor state policy alone will solve our problems—one wonders why there was so much argument about something so basic. We can live without neither the activists nor the entrepreneurs and in a vicious climate, before an election where everyone seems to be reflecting their own agenda, at least we, the voters, must take a step back, try to look at the whole picture, and then vote.

2. What They See From the Hill

When the car of the Indian Member of Parliament (MP) snakes towards work every day, often it turns towards a broad, pond-lined avenue at the heart of the Indian capital. Often in the ponds, there are ducks, dingy boats and children. There are ice-cream vendors at the traffic signal where, about forty years ago, the prime minister's son and daughter-in-law stopped for ice-cream and made an immortal photo of the normalcy of the monarchs.

The avenue is called Rajpath, Avenue of Kings, and unlike the Avenue des Champs-Elysees in Paris, does not have luxury shops on two sides. No Louis Vuitton or Gucci clouds the scenic view of the Indian MP. Nor can one see a permanent protest ground opposite it, in the manner of Lafayette Square vis-à-vis the White House. India's evergreen protest maidan is tucked away in an alley in front of a medieval solar observatory, Jantar Mantar. The Indian MP never passes it on his way to work, though it is within 10 kilometres from Parliament.

The cars, usually with a red beacon bulb on top, fly by, unstopped and usually unstoppable, in memory of a simpler time when there was only one television channel and socializing with politicians was unthinkable. These days, unless you are the prime minister, or the president, the entourage of the MP might actually stop at a traffic light. If the Member of Parliament is slightly image-conscious, the siren with the beacon will go unused. Things have a nasty way of turning infectious and viral these days on computers and mobile phones. It's a disease, sighs the siren-less MP.

But overall these are happy surrounds. As they sweep in towards their private hall of fame each morning, the Indian MP sees no commotion, none of the blister and bustle of a 1.2 billion bustling country. Here on Rajpath and up the giddy smooth neck of Raisina Hill, the Indian MP finds tranquillity, a Vipassana-like calm as the noise of the country fades behind them and before them rises the sublime peace of complete power. Nothing bad could ever happen to them here.

We know that they don't care

No study has shown how far away India's rulers—for that is what they are, not representatives but rulers—are from those they lord upon, but it is a fact that every Indian instinctively knows in their hearts. We know that they don't care. Now this does not mean that there aren't numerous, extremely hard-working, conscientious, austere Members of Parliament, but we are talking here about the public impression, the image—some would say cultivated by years of negligence—of the institution and many of those who inhabit it, and have in the past.

The image that many such MPs have created is such that today when we see the rise of Raisina Hill, we know they are too far away.

3. Whose Time Has Come

Every minute of running Parliament costs us, the people of India, Rs 2.5 lakh. How do we know this? Because former Parliamentary Affairs Minister (later ousted under bribe clouds) Pawan Kumar Bansal told us so in the Rajya Sabha in September 2012.

Why was he saying this? Because in that monsoon session of Parliament, the Lok Sabha worked for only 20 per cent of the total allocated time and the Rajya Sabha only for 27 per cent of the scheduled hours.

At the end of this session, 102 bills were pending and only 4 bills had been passed.

This monsoon session was followed by a winter session of Parliament where the Lok Sabha sat for 61 hours and 45 minutes—but wasted 59 hours and 7 minutes screaming and shouting, a meaningless activity that was politely referred to as 'interruptions' by Speaker Meira Kumar, who said only 49 of the 400 listed questions could be answered at the rate of 2.45 questions a day. I am

The Lok Sabha sat for 61 hours and 45 minutes—but wasted 59 hours and 7 minutes

not sure how you answer 0.45 of a question but then I am not a Member of Parliament.

Now what does this mean in terms of money wasted? (In case you have forgotten, this is the tax payer's money, our money—yours and mine—that is being wasted.)

59 hours x 2.5 lakh x 60 minutes = Rs 88.50 crore. What can Rs 88 crore buy? Well, Rs 88 crore is what the Punjab government sanctioned in 2013 for the upgrade of government colleges.

In the Rajya Sabha, during that winter of discontent, 47 hours of a total of 57 hours were wasted.

In 2013, the Indian Parliament met for its monsoon session in inclement weather; the currency need resuscitation, a pathologically violent society needed to be addressed and international condemnation for economic despair needed to be faced.

This was going to be one of the most critical sessions of Parliament before the 2014 elections and two critical bills considered voter friendly were passed—the National Food Security Bill and the Right to Fair Compensation and Transparency in Land Acquisition, Rehabilitation and Resettlement Bill—and one amendment allowing MPs to retain their seat during appeal after a criminal conviction was attempted to be passed (until the rage of Rahul Gandhi sort of tore that apart).

How much time did they waste then? PRS Legislative Research, the foundation that tracks Parliament with all the stealth and accuracy of a jungle cat, says even with all the hectic action—many noticed that this was one of the most productive parliament sessions in recent times—the Lok Sabha wasted 42 per cent of its scheduled time and the Rajya Sabha 20 per cent. And even in the time used, only 53 per cent was spent discussing legislations.

18 of 170 pending bills were cleared.

This sort of wastage of legislative time and resources is not new. It has been going on for years. In fact, even in 2011, one exasperated Member of Parliament, Shashi Tharoor, a relatively new politician and therefore perhaps less willing to remain self-servingly silent, wrote that the British parliamentary system in India had outlived its purpose and 'our parliamentary system has created a unique breed of legislator, largely unqualified to legislate, who has sought election only in order to wield (or influence) executive power'. (By the way, Tharoor's worry is not new. B.K. Nehru, Indian diplomat and nephew of Jawaharlal Nehru, was an early proponent of the presidential system. In the BJP, L.K. Advani, and Arun Shourie, have been champions of the thought that a change in the system is necessary.)

In 2014, unless there is a clear, resounding verdict, Tharoor's dystopian nightmare 'what will happen if the next election produces a Parliament of 30-odd parties jostling to see which permutation of their numbers will get them the best rewards' could well come true.

Remember that former prime minister, Atal Bihari Vajpayee of the BJP, warned us of this when he used to speak in Parliament about the 'ekla chalo re' phenomenon of one member, single person Indian 'political parties' who use bitter bargaining power in a coalition government purely for private loot.

4. When in Doubt

The first Member of Parliament who complained bitterly to me about having to 'meet criminals every day' was the Bengali bard, Kabir Suman. In 2009, right after the polls, I met the singer of songs, so melancholic that they are described as 'soulful', outside Parliament. He was smoking a cigarette. His other complaint was 'when I heard the pay, I felt like it was pushing people to be corrupt'.

It is perhaps pertinent to point out, that he was a first time MP.

I don't know how many more MPs feel this way but a year later in 2010, salaries of Indian MPs (tax free) went up to Rs 50,000 a month from Rs 16,000. The *Times of India* calculated that, at that time, this was 68 times the average monthly earning of an Indian. They also doubled their constituency and office expenses to Rs 40,000, and the repayable advance for buying a car went up from Rs 100,000 to Rs 400,000. The daily allowance for attending Parliament also doubled to Rs 2,000 a day.

The road mileage per kilometre went up from Rs 13 to Rs 16.

This apart from the free water, electricity, severely subsidised housing—in some of the most expensive real estate in the world, that is, Lutyens' Delhi—unlimited first class rail travel and a limited amount of business class air travel.

MPs can travel for free in business class to attend sessions of Parliament, consultative and standing committee meetings etc. Apart from this, they get another 34 business class tickets which can be used by them or their companion or spouse. At least eight times, the ticket can be used by the companion or spouse even if the MP is not travelling with them. What happens to unused tickets? They get carried to the following year.

There are other perks too. Like the 'washing allowance' for the cost of washing sofa covers and curtains which is given once in three months and a furniture allowance of Rs 60,000 a year for durable furniture and Rs 15,000 for non-durable furniture.

At the same time, free telephone calls went up from 100,000 to 150,000. Their homes also get 4,000 kilolitres of water and 50,000 units of electricity a year for free and reimbursement on money spent on tiles for the kitchen and the bathrooms.

What happens when a Member of Parliament is no longer a Member of Parliament? Well, they used to get Rs 8,000 a month as pension. That doubled to Rs 20,000 a month in 2010.

Did you know? The MPs had asked for the pay raise to be Rs 80,001—or one rupee more than the salary of the cabinet secretary. One of the most ardent supporters of this Re 1 difference was reportedly the Congress MP, Bhakta Charan Das who is also the MP from the Niyamgiri region of Odisha and the man who helped organise Rahul Gandhi's famous speech supporting the villagers. I suppose he wanted the cabinet secretary to be clear about the hierarchy.

Even as I am writing this, Lalu Yadav of the Rashtriya Janata Dal (RJD), he who was to remain omnipresent like the aloo in the samosa, is headed to prison, also losing his MP status and ability to contest polls for a decade at least, convicted in one of the six cases of the Rs 950 crore fodder fund theft. But he would not be the first one. Rasheed Masood from the Congress has already got a sentence of four years for fraudulently giving admission to students in medical colleges.

Now the Association for Democratic Reforms (ADR) says at least 72 sitting MPs could go to prison and be disqualified if they were only convicted; 18 of these are from the Bharatiya Janata Party (BJP), 14 from the Congress, 8 from the Samajwadi Party, 6 from the Bahujan Samaj Party, 4 from the All India Anna Dravida Munnetra Kazhagam (AIADMK), 3 from the Janata Dal-United (JD-U) and 2 from the Communist Party of India-Marxist (CPI-M), and 17 from other small parties.

According to ADR, 30 per cent of all MPs in the Lok Sabha and 17 per cent in the Rajya Sabha have criminal cases against them. These crimes range between petty and serious. Some MPs have criminal cases (like theft, forgery, embezzlement, bribe)—and others have grave criminal cases (rape, murder, inciting riots).

In the Lok Sabha, among those with criminal records, 14 per cent had serious cases against them. The percentage for the Rajya Sabha was 7 per cent. Presumably, the house of nominated elders was more benign than the house directly elected through rough and tumble youngers.

And what were the political parties doing about such candidates? Sending them back to Parliament, of course. ADR's research showed 74 per cent of MPs who had criminal cases were given a ticket to contest a second time. ADR looked at the criminal records of 4,181 repeat candidates and showed that 1,072 had criminal cases the first time they contested an election and 788 had cases during the second time. This means political parties gave tickets to 74 per cent of candidates with criminal records the second time, despite having information on their criminal background from previous elections. But the total number of candidates with criminal cases still increased the second time as there were 507 other candidates (out of 4,181) who showed no criminal cases in the first election but declared cases in the second round of elections. Therefore the total share of candidates with criminal records given tickets by political parties rose from 26 per cent to 31 per cent.

What happened with candidates with serious criminal cases? Well, of 540 candidates with serious charges, 353 or 65 per cent were given tickets for the second time. Then there were 289 other candidates with no criminal cases in the first election, but who had declared cases in the second round of elections. This also shows that the total share of candidates with serious criminal records given tickets by political parties rose from 12 per cent to 15 per cent.

Funnily enough, statistics showed that MPs with criminal records won polls more often than their clean colleagues!

So where is Kabir Suman these days? With such out of the box distaste for parliamentary shenanigans, he naturally fought with his party—the Trinamool Congress—and having fallen out of favour, leads the quiet life of the estranged MP.

Hope? Congress Vice President Rahul Gandhi's words and some activism by Member of Parliament Milind Deora prevented a legislation that would protect MPs accused of crime. The process of kicking them out of Parliament has started with Rasheed Masood (Congress, Rajya Sabha) and Lalu Yadav (Rashtriya Janata Dal, Lok Sabha). The question is—will this sustain? Will the clean up last?

Just when we were beginning to cheer, we received news that

Statistics showed that MPs with criminal records won polls more often than their clean colleagues!

Bahujan Samaj Party MP, Dhananjay Singh (who once had more than two dozen cases against him including murder and 'double murder) and his second wife, Jagriti Singh, were accused, following the death of their maid inside their MP bungalow in a series of cases, including murder, attempt to murder, the Bonded Labour Act and the Juvenile Justice Act.

Is it not time that we ask—why are they there? Are we reasonably sure that the one we vote for will actually legislate? If not, is there someone else we ought to vote for?

5. Return on Investment

Have you heard of Dr. Mahendra Prasad? He is, according to the Rajya Sabha website, an 'environmentalist, horticulturist, agriculturist, political and social worker'. He is a member of the Rajya Sabha courtesy the Janata Dal (United), the ruling party in Bihar.

He is also India's richest member of Parliament—a pharmaceutical tycoon worth Rs 683 crore. He owns a company called Aristo Pharmaceuticals which is said to be worth Rs 5,000 crore but there are very few details available about it. He is from the Jehanabad district of Bihar, home to some of the bloodiest fighting between the Naxal rebels and private landlord armies in the late 1990s.

He was entered in the Limca Book of Records as the most travelled parliamentarian between 2004 and 2011, having visited 206 countries including Marshall Islands, Nauru and Suriname, also Fiji and El Salvador thrice each and Ethiopia five times.

No matter who rules in Bihar—Lalu Yadav's RJD or Nitish Kumar's JD-U—Prasad remains in the Rajya Sabha.

In 2009, when the new Lok Sabha came in, 315 out of 543 members were worth more than Rs 1 crore. According to some calculations, the entire house was worth more than Rs 3,000 crore. Even taking into account that some of the MPs owned real estate assets whose prices had soared, India's parliamentarians were hardly lacking in personal funds.

Andhra Pradesh sent in the wealthiest parliamentarians, headed by Jagan Reddy—then with the Congress, now leader of his breakaway party—who was worth Rs 445 crore. Then there was Nama Nageshwara Rao of the Telegu Desam Party who brought in Rs 174 crore (he owns an infrastructure company called Madhucon Projects). The state had two super rich parliamentarians in Rajya Sabha too—the indefatigable Subbarami Reddy, renowned for his parties, and in the Rajya Sabha via the Congress (Rs 258 crore) and Yalamanchili Satyanarayana Chowdary who had around Rs 190 crore (owner of the Sujana group of companies which makes fans among other things).

ADR pointed out that if you were to compare the riches of MPs who were elected in 2004 and 2009, their wealth went up in this period by 289 per cent.

Just to give a sense of proportion between the 2004 and 2009 Lok Sabha, there were 156 crorepatis or members who had assets of more than Rs 1 crore. The number went up by 102 per cent to 315, as we mentioned before, by the time the results rolled in five years later.

The average asset of an MP in the Lok Sabha in 2004 was Rs 0.86 crore (or Rs 86 lakh). This went up to Rs 5.33 crore in 2009.

According to ADR, out of the 4,181 candidates who contested more than one election, 3,173 showed an increase in wealth. The average increase in wealth of all 4,181 recontesting candidates has been Rs 2.34 crore. The average assets of these 4,181 recontesting candidates has grown from Rs 1.74 crore to Rs 4.08 crore.

Of recontesting candidates, 1,615 candidates showed an

increase of more than 200 per cent in wealth, 684 showed an increase of over 500 per cent, 420 of over 800 per cent and 317 of over 1000 per cent.

The average asset of an MP in the Lok Sabha in 2004 was Rs 0.86 crore (or Rs 86 lakh). This went up to Rs 5.33 crore in 2009

The understated ADR says: 'This is clearly an abnormal increase in wealth.'

Of course MPs are not the only politicians who seem to find politics lucrative. There are Members of Legislative Assemblies (MLA) too who are not too badly off. One fine example is a man called Venod Sharma. You may have heard about him. A Congressman from Ambala in Haryana, he is the father of the imprisoned Manu Sharma, convicted for the murder of model, Jessica Lall. Well, in spite of his troubles, his declared—please remember that we are only discussing declared assets here—rose from Rs 9 crore in 2004 to Rs 87 crore in 2009.

Here's another tale I like—this one from erstwhile royalty no less, the Nawab, it seems like he still calls himself Nawab—of Rampur Kazim Ali Khan's assets rose from Rs 9 crore in 2007 to Rs 56 crore in 2012 when he was an MLA from Suar.

Shouldn't we debate how so many of our politicians are able to inflate their income and assets as soon as they are elected?

As Alice said in Wonderland, 'of ships, and seals, and sealing wax, and cabbages and kings / And if the sea is boiling hot, and whether pigs have wings'. Sometimes they do.

6. In God We Trust, Everyone Else Brings Security

There are 14,842 special people in India, mostly politicians, who get state security. This at a time when India and its states spend Rs 2 lakh crore and still have a shortfall of, according to India Spend—the data journalism organisation—half a million people.

But these strained police resources still provide 47,000 cops to protect VIPs. Three states—Uttar Pradesh, Maharashtra and Gujarat—have the highest number of cops scheduled on duty protecting these important people.

Uttar Pradesh, Maharashtra and Gujarat have the highest number of cops protecting VIPs

According to the Bureau of Police Research and Development, Uttar Pradesh and Gujarat are two states that have the maximum difference between sanctioned strength of their police force and actual feet on the ground. Uttar Pradesh has barely about half the strength on the streets and Gujarat just a bit more.

There are various levels of security in India. At the top is Special Protection Group (SPG) which protects the prime minister of India, former prime ministers and their immediate family members. The SPG has a force of 3,500 people. It was created to guard prime ministers and their family members after the assassination of Indira Gandhi by her own bodyguards. The decision to extend the SPG cover to former prime ministers came after it was removed for Rajiv Gandhi and who was, like his mother, assassinated. Then there is the more than 14,000-strong National Security Guard (NSG), an anti-terrorism force, which has various levels—Z+ (38 member strong security team), Z (26 people), Y (11) and X (2). Narendra Modi, who faces one of the highest threats, has a three-tier security cover of 108 NSG Black Cat commandos.

Two of the latest people who joined the Z+ level were Steel Minister, Beni Prasad Verma of the Congress Party, and Bahujan Samaj Party MP Brajesh Pathak who, as the Association of Democratic Reforms noted, had been accused of several crimes, including murder and rioting.

Two others from the Congress-friendly Uttar Pradesh constituencies of Rae Bareli and Amethi, MLAs Haji Haroon Rashid, a petrol pump owner, and Mohammad Muslim, bagged Y level cover, after Sushil Kumar Shinde took over the home ministry from P. Chidambaram who was trying to reduce such covers across the board.

Curiously a member of the National Integration Council, Udit Raj, has Y level security, as does a former tourism minister Subodh Kant Sahai. You know you ought to be really worried when members of national integration councils and ex-tourism ministers need security.

7. Wander Lust

The LTC sounds like a drug; it isn't, but could be. It is sometimes called LTA, which makes it sound paternal, like a parent-teacher meeting. The LTA is Leave Travel Allowance.

In early 2013, the Central Vigilance Commission discovered some of our parliamentarians were gobbling up the LTCs like there was no tomorrow. It said at least nine members of the Rajya Sabha were involved in scamming with travel agents to inflate air fare bills, produce false tickets and show business class travel for reimbursement when they actually only travelled economy.

One of the prime accused was Anil Kumar Sahani of the Janata Dal-United (JD-U), who was reported to have come up with at least eight business class tickets worth Rs 150,000 each, but investigations revealed that actually the boarding cards belonged to two other people.

Of course the honourable MPs have sometimes drawn example of love for travel from the very top. The former president Pratibha Patil—after having spent Rs 205 crore on 12 foreign trips in her five-year period—

Pratibha Patil spent Rs 205 crore on 12 foreign trips in her five-year period

popped across to South Africa and Seychelles just before leaving office spending a quickfire Rs 18 crore. Recently, 30 Karnataka MLAs planned a trip to 'study' Amazon rainforests. The cost? Rs 7.5 lakh per head. How much of this travelling is helping us, the people?

8. The MP and the iPad

No matter what model you choose, an iPad weighs less than 1 kilogramme. That's substantially less than 3 kilogrammes, figured Vice President and Chairman of the Rajya Sabha, Hamid Ansari.

His assigned committee, headed by then Rajya Sabha Secretary General, V. K. Agnihotri, discovered that each member of the Rajya Sabha was getting between 1 and 3 kilogrammes of paper documents every day—everything from legislative bills, questions and answers, notices, even printed menus from the eateries in Parliament.

And so it was that the Rajya Sabha MPs, and their bretheren in the Lok Sabha, got Rs 50,000 to buy an iPad (or if they so choose, a Samsung Galaxy Tab).

Now one is not quite sure by what amount this has brought down the paper piles in Parliament but there is one way to try and understand the technological embrace of our politicians and parliamentarians. It is interesting that the entire conversation of politics on social media in India is seen through the prism of adoption and not use.

We are very concerned about who is appearing on Facebook

and Twitter and what they are saying there, but almost never bothered about what the politicians actually do on these platforms.

There is one reason for this. We are used to a system where politicians have no accountability and we have no access to them. What has happened with social media is the same thing that happens with people who appear frequently on television and film stars and the public at large. You feel that you know these people, who have a say, even though you actually don't.

For a country used to a relationship of distance and servility with the people in charge, even this small sense access is overwhelming, and therefore our collective excitement that we can—fascinatingly—actually see what our politicians are thinking minute to minute, day to day. Even if that access is completely controlled and curated by them, not us.

That's why perhaps it is time we need to measure social media activity by politicians on the critical factor of interactivity. How much do politicians interact with the people? Now the immediate counterpoint to this would be that politicians with large numbers of followers would naturally also draw many trolls and abusive, irrelevant comments.

But that argument does not entirely hold true if you study the threads of most Indian politicians. You will notice one common thing—most of them use social media like a loud speaker. It amplifies what they want to say to many, many people but like with the pamphlets and the loudspeakers, no questions can be asked, no answers

Most social media platforms used by politicians in India are not social at all for it is not a conversation. It is a monologue. Can we get them to converse and respond?

offered. Most social media platforms used by politicians in India are not social at all for it is not a conversation. It is a monologue. Can we get them to converse and respond?

I got some evidence of this from @netaspeak—an account that my open government foundation *Whypoll* created, to curate a daily question and answer between people and politicians. We defined our job as merely this—no abuse, no trolling but relevant serious questions every day to politicians on Twitter. We wanted to create a sense of conversation on governance. We believed it would ease some of the acute trust deficit that Indian politics faces today.

Almost immediately, we realised that none of the biggest politicians ever reply. Rahul Gandhi (@BewithRG, there is some confusion on whether this is the account that Gandhi uses but among the many on his name, this seems to be the best updated with serious and verifiable information) does not. Nor does Narendra Modi (@narendramodi). Sharad Pawar (@Pawar_Sharad) does not. Nor does Sushma Swaraj (@SushmaSwarajbjp) (though at least she has engaging conversations with fellow politician tweeple like Jammu and Kashmir Chief Minister, Omar Abdullah, who is at @abdullah_omar). None of the chief ministers—from Mamata Banerjee (not from any of the three accounts in her name), Nitish Kumar (@NitishKumarJDU), Ashok Gehlot (@ashokgehlot51), Shivraj Singh Chouhan (@ChouhanShivraj), Oomen Chandy (@ Oomen_Chandy) to Manohar Parrikar (@manoharparrikar)—actually ever respond.

Nor do most of the Members of Parliament. In fact, the Twitter account of Manish Tewari, the minister in charge for information and broadcasting, is actually protected! You cannot immediately follow him or see his tweets. A request has to be sent for you to be vetoed and approved to follow him. Is it not curious that the minister for information and broadcasting should have a protected Twitter feed? Isn't that an odd sign of open government? Surely someone in his office can scan and filter out the trolls and abuse?

We realised how serious this question of openness on social media is when @netaspeak was blocked by the account of the prime minister @PMOIndia. Why? Did we abuse? Troll the account of the prime minister's office?

No.

This is what happened. The economist Surjit Bhalla wrote an article in the *Financial Express* where he challenged the official government estimates on the Food Security Bill. The combative economist, who had been accused of 'molesting' data to prove his point by Biraj Patnaik, the food expert and Principal Adviser to the Commissioners of the Supreme Court, said this as the last paragraph of his piece:

'This is an open challenge to Ms Sonia, and Dr Manmohan Singh and Mr P Chidambaram. Your minions are stating that the ordinance induced FSB will only increase by about 25 per cent and will amount to 1 per cent of GDP. I get a conservative increase of 336 per cent, or a total subsidy level of 3 per cent of GDP with an honest implementation of the Bill, sorry ordinance. One of us is massively wrong. I believe it is not me. But prove it otherwise.'

To which, @netaspeak asked on Twitter, who is wrong, who is lying about the data—the PMO or Surjit Bhalla?

We asked this to the Twitter account of the PMO, Congress Spokesperson Digvijay Singh and Pankaj Pachauri, the communications adviser to the prime minister. To begin with, we were delighted that Pachauri wrote back, tagging Bhalla and pointing to a piece written by Swaminathan A. Aiyar, the veteran economic journalist.

We immediately tweeted back a thank you saying very

pleasantly surprised to see a response. 'Kudos for the response', we wrote.

Then, we were blocked from the accounts of both the PMO and Pachauri. And in spite of many protestations on Twitter, we remain blocked. We don't know why.

But there is some hope in this space.

Shashi Tharoor, who often says that he has learnt from personal experience of the 'cattle class controversy' on what to say and what not to say on Twitter, continues to be effervescent and forthcoming, if more guarded than before, with responses, and that has not changed much whether he is an MP or minister. Baijayant Panda of the Biju Janata Dal (BJD) retains a delicious sense of humour and responds. Omar Abdullah can be quite forthcoming and none of his tweets sound like a slogan.

But they are the exceptions that prove the rule that the Indian politician loves only the sound of their own voice—even when tweeting.

Will having a paid-for iPad (or Tab) change that? No. We can only hope that it will.

9. Right to Reject? NOT(A) Quite

Au contraire to popular belief, India's right to reject passed by the Supreme Court does not mean that voters can dismiss all candidates in a constituency and force a re-election. Since this will be an election of four letter words—RaGa, NaMo—the right to reject has given us one more. NOTA, or None Of The Above.

This means that no matter how many NOTA votes are cast, even if most of the votes cast in a constituency are NOTA, a candidate winning the few remaining minority votes would be declared elected.

Unless the law is amended to say that if majority of the votes cast are NOTA, a re-election needs to be held, this does not solve the problem of corrupt candidates. It does push parties to reform their selection of candidates but not enough. As it often is in India, this rule does not go all the way.

The NOTA only makes an existing rule simpler. This is Section 49 (O) of the Conduct of Elections Rules, 1961 which gives voters the right to not vote and fill in a

Now there is going to be a NOTA button. Use it. But remember it's the beginning of change, not the end

register instead to say that they reject all candidates. Their finger is still inked so that their vote cannot be misused.

Often, unless one was particularly ardent like some voters in Mumbai were in the city's last municipal polls, Section 49 (O) would never be used.

Now there is going to be a NOTA button. Use it. But remember it's the beginning of change, not the end.

10. The Toilets of Modern India

We know that we have more mobile phones than toilets in India. But what's the actual shortfall and how many have we been building?

The United Nations says that by 2008, about 336 million people had 'access to improved sanitation', which means they were not defecating in the open, on the road, on the rail tracks or behind the bush.

The Planning Commission came up with an Evaluation Study on Total Sanitation Campaign in 2013. This study covered 11,519 households across 27 states—which means this was what is called a comprehensive survey, something you can trust.

What was one of the big things that this survey found?

Well, that 72.63 per cent of all rural households 'practice open defecation'—basically they relieve themselves behind the bushes, on railway tracks, wherever they feel is fine.

How does it help if people are shitting in toilets rather than under the fine open skies listening to birds chirping? The survey has an answer. Seems like if a gram panchayat has won the status of Nirmal Gram Panchayat or a place where no one 'practices open defecation, cases of illness in those families fell from 0.26

to 0.17, or by 35 per cent. Also, 88 per cent of such households told the surveyors that they felt that their 'general well being' had improved and 96 per cent said that women in their household felt more secure.

So why aren't more people switching to building and using toilets? The report says two reasons:

- they don't have enough information about how to do this and why it is beneficial.
- they are just too set in the old ways or 'age old practice'.

Even in places that there are toilets, there doesn't seem to be a complete toilet. Apart from the states of Karnataka, Kerala, Sikkim, Tamil Nadu, Haryana and Gujarat, toilets in the villages of every other state have either the roof missing or one (or more) of the four walls, or the depth of the pit is not right.

In total, only 59 per cent of toilets in areas surveyed had the full, complete structure.

The worst performer? West Bengal with only 12.3 per cent complete toilets to Sikkim where 99 per cent of the toilets were complete.

Now, even when you have toilets, often there is no water!

Only 46 per cent of the households surveyed had water for flushing and—hear this—only 3.61 per cent had water on the tap (or maybe a tap at all).

So how are our states divided in this?

At the top are states where mostly there are toilets—Sikkim (100 per cent), Kerala (95.4 per cent), Haryana (86.6 per cent), West Bengal (83.5 per cent, most of them might not be complete, but at least they are there and can be used) and Tamil Nadu (76.4 per cent).

Then there are states like Gujarat, Uttar Pradesh, Assam, Manipur, Andhra Pradesh, Maharashtra and Uttarakhand which score between 50 per cent and 70 per cent.

At the bottom is Bihar with 23.4 per cent.

Now what else is critical about this toilets issue? Well, for one, toilets go a long way, perhaps even much longer that the Food Security Bill, in seriously battling malnutrition. To put it in a nutshell—death by diarrhoea.

How many children are underweight and stunted in India?

According to the Public Health Association, only about half of all Indians wash their hands with soap after defecation

Unicef says 61.7 million. The Ministry of Statistics and Programme Implementation calculated in 2012 that 20 per cent of all Indian children under five years of age are underweight and malnourished.

Now the World Health Organisation says one of the main causes of malnutrition among kids under the age of five is diarrhoea.

Poor sanitation leads to diarrhoea.

According to the Public Health Association, only about half of all Indians wash their hands with soap after defecation.

Unicef India says just the act of washing hands with soap after visiting the bathroom would bring down diarrhoeal deaths in India by 40 per cent. At the moment, one in every four child dying of diarrhoea around the world (about 800,000 of them each year) comes from India. So 25 per cent of all the children dying of diarrhoea around the world come from just our country.

And how many of the kids with diarrhoea in India are washing their hands with soap? Only 20 per cent. The remaining do not wash their hands with soap—the one thing that could easily keep them alive.

Still want to feel proud that we have more mobile phones than toilets? Yes, Narendra Modi has said that he thinks toilets should be built before temples and yes, Jairam Ramesh has been crying hoarse about how important this issue is, but it might also be worth checking out what your MP thinks about this.

11. Ever Heard of the Library Scandal?

You have heard of the 2G telecom scam, the Commonwealth Games scam, the coal mining scandal—and we shall come to all that in a bit—but have you ever heard of the library scandal?

In 2010-11, a report was published by the famous (or infamous) Comptroller and Auditor General (CAG) of India on the state of affairs at the country's main documentation centre—the National Library.

What's the budget of the National Library? Between 2003 and 2009, the National Library had an allocated budget of Rs 112.30 crore. They spent about Rs 106.10 crore of this or 94 per cent.

After having spent 94 per cent of their budget, what did they achieve?

Here are the main findings of the CAG:

- By law, the National Library is supposed to get a free copy of every book published by every publisher in India. That's right, every book from every publisher. There's a law which says this. It's called the Delivery of Books and Newspaper (Public Libraries) Act of 1954. This is, as the

CAG points out, the primary reason the National Library exists; this acquisition, documentation and storage is its raison d'etre. But—and there's a big but here—in reality, depending on the year being audited, the library only got between 5 per cent and 26 per cent of the books. Even though the library can take legal action against publishers who fail to send books, it never does. Basically no one cared or bothered. (Does that sound familiar in our country?)

So the good people of the CAG even gave a list of the worst offenders among the publishers. There are thirteen names on that list—from really big names like Rupa, Penguin and Roli to smaller publishers like Anu Books, New Age Books and KSK Publishers.

There's more.

- The CAG had something to say about the way the National Library bought its foreign publications. It called the system of purchase 'neither transparent and competitive, nor directed by any need-based approach to cover gaps in the existing collection'.
- Now, even when the library did receive books, what did it do? 'Inordinate delay in processing of books deprived readers of the benefit of an estimated 300,000 books which could not reach the shelves.' In foreign languages, only books from 5 out of 58 languages could be processed.
- And what about rare books? Most of them were exposed to damage or theft, said the CAG, including letters of Subhash Chandra Bose,

Even though the library can take legal action against publishers who fail to send books, it never does

Rabindranath Tagore and Sarojini Naidu, manuscripts which were more than hundred years old and even the priceless world's smallest dictionary.

- With unique Indian efficiency, the National Library had been able to digitize only 9,141 books in 10 years and less than 1 per cent of rare newspapers more than 100 years old could be microfilmed.

Do you remember politicians talking about whether they have a plan to rescue and restore our priceless heritage while asking for votes? Don't you think they should have a plan?

12. Be Afraid

Something good happened in India in 2012. For the first time since 1994—which means for the first time since terror came to the Kashmir valley in 1989—deaths from terrorism fell to three digits.

According to the South Asia Terrorism Monitor, which tracks such things, one of the worst years in recent times was 2001 when 5,839 people were killed. This fell to 1,073 in 2011 and then to 804 in 2012.

Jammu and Kashmir had the least number of deaths (117) in 2012, significantly lower than 183 in 2011 and 4,507 in the peak violence year of 2001.

Even Maoist violence is down from 1,080 fatalities in 2010, dramatically dropping to 602 in 2011, and then 367 in 2012.

What caused this? Depending on who you ask, the answers will vary—increased push of government developmental work, extravagant ambition of the Maoists that pushed them out of their natural habitats and into security forces gunfire, Pakistan's preoccupation with fighting its own terrorists and Taliban spill-overs from Afghanistan, tough action against terror cells by the Sheikh Hasina-led Bangladesh government, thinning support for rebels due to rising aspiration for jobs and middleclass-dom among local populations who prefer to migrate to towns and cities and seek urban lifestyles and culture and as everyone knows no guerilla war can survive without local support and cover.

The point is—the numbers are down.

What we have then is a rare window of opportunity—which we are likely to blow with incompetence and imbecility. Take Kashmir. I went to the valley several times in 2013 and each time, the people I spoke to—shopkeepers, students, teachers, bankers, hydro-electric plant managers, walnut wood carvers, shawl embroiderers, government employees, computer engineers, call centre executives, saffron and lavender sellers, politicians—expressed the desire to do something. Be someone. Change their lives. Not dependent on government. Use their enterprise. All they needed was a bit of facilitation.

Does this mean that tomorrow, propelled by entrepreneurs, the Kashmir problem will be solved? Of course not. There are too many stakeholders and rent seekers from the violence—from corrupt politicians on both sides of the border, crooked separatists and vile security forces of two countries who benefit by the continuing violence—but today more than ever the purchase of the militancy argument is weak and grows weaker still each day.

It is a moment when there seems to be a generational and emotional transformation taking place in Kashmir. It is a time when the idea of progress, the idea of self-fulfilment would be embraced with vigour, especially if India can show what peace can achieve, what magic jobs, prosperity and respect brings.

That means—as one young entrepreneur told me—when the finance minister of India comes to Kashmir, let him not talk just to the old politicians, let him also talk to the people.

When the finance minister of India comes to Kashmir, let him not talk just to the old politicians, let him also talk to the people

They will tell him to notice all the things that have been achieved even though they barely get 200 normal working days in Kashmir. If the finance minister could figure out a way to defend the people from militants and keep the army largely out of sight on a day to day basis then they will show him what they can do.

To understand this I spoke to two veteran Kashmiris. One, the renowned former head of the Jammu and Kashmir Bank, Haseeb Drabu and the other, perhaps Kashmir's best known woman entrepreneur, Gazalla Amin.

'The valley is cut away from public sentiment about the 2014 elections in the rest of India,' said Drabu. 'People say why do we care whether it is Modi or Gandhi? How will our lives change?'

He has a radical idea which he believes would make the 2014 elections unique for his state. 'If Narendra Modi were to go to Kashmir—not Jammu but first to Kashmir—and declare that Article 370 (which gives the state special status in the Indian union) is dead, now that would be a move forward. The Kashmiris know that 370 is anyway dead. Dragging its myth bears no fruit. The people of Kashmir are tired of status quo, tired of things being as they are.

'But if he goes to Jammu first, immediately there will only be deeper polarisation. Already there is a lot of polarisation. Someone needs to break that.'

As it so happened, Modi went to Jammu first and asked how Article 370 had been beneficial to the state. To that, Drabu has a nuanced answer. It isn't that he is per se against Article 370.

As an economist, he points out its many benefits. Land reforms happened in Kashmir aided by Article 370 and because of that the state has wonderfully low numbers of landless labourers and overall poor people including rural poor. His point is that relentless collusion between political leaders in the valley and central government has made Article 370 increasingly toothless and a mere political tool, a gimmick, a charade. And he would like someone brazen like Modi to shake up the system, break down some old charades and renegotiate Kashmir's special status afresh.

Gazalla Amin, sometimes called the lavender queen of Kashmir for her ever expanding business in perfume oils, says most Kashmiris are worried. 'When the US pulls out of Afghanistan, we believe the focus will be Kashmir again. The rumour is already Kashmir is getting militants crossing over from Afghanistan.'

She says she worries about extremist elements from across the border in Pakistan threatening to reopen the war in Kashmir after the Americans withdraw from Afghanistan. 'If we are really such an integral part of India, what is the government doing to protect us?' Amin says the fear of militancy exploding is once again a vital fear in the Valley. 'Once we were promised a referendum but that will never happen. But how can you argue that we are such an integral part of India unless you send the army back to the barracks? Send them back to the barracks, show us a plan to fight militants crossing the border; let us feel that the state of India protects us! That's how the elections will really speak to us.'

But that won't be easy. Some of India's most protracted problems remain. In September 2013, one Hafiz Saeed was reported to have said in Islamabad that jihad against India will continue unless Kashmir is 'freed'.

In a tweet on 6 September 2013, Saeed (@HafizSaeedJUD), who India suspects is the mastermind behind the 26/11 terror attacks in Mumbai which killed at least 164 people, said about Kashmir and the common Indian statement that it is an *atoot angh* or irretrievable part of India: 'If India insists on *atoot angh*—then every *angh* is at the risk of being shattered. Taking one's right is not terrorism.'

This at a time when South Asia security experts worry that the destination of the Afghan jihad will be Kashmir after NATO forces withdraw from Afghanistan in 2014.

Then there is the east where in 2012, violence between the Bodo tribesmen and Bengalis in Assam left 80 dead and 400,000–500,000 people displaced within the state, the largest involuntary movement of people within India since independence.

On 12 July 2005, K.P.S. Gill, the man who fought and won against militancy in Punjab, pointed out that, according to the Supreme Court of India, Assam was facing 'external aggression and internal disturbance' on account of the large-scale illegal influx of Bangladeshi migrants, and that it was 'the duty of the union of India to take all measures for protection of the state of Assam from such external aggression and internal disturbance as enjoined in Article 355 of the Constitution.'

Now there are varying narratives to this. The Assam government says illegal migration is actually thinning and most of the Muslim population increase in the state is due to the large families in the community due to 'illiteracy'. And the data from the UN Department of Economic and Social Affairs (UN-DESA) says that in 2013, India was home to 3.2 million Bangladeshi migrants—'the single largest bilateral stock of international migrants' in the developing world.

Now this per se is not worrying. After all, even if you leave aside substantial Indian populations in the Western world, in the

United Arab Emirates there are 2.9 million Indian migrants and 1.8 million in Saudi Arabia. You have to stop being scared just by numbers.

The question is does India's border with Bangladesh, which is sometimes described as a porous or near open border with constant traffic, pose a security threat? Well, India's parliamentarians certainly think so. In 2008, a Parliamentary Standing Committee on Home Affairs warned us on large numbers of fake rupees entering India through some illegal migrants and many of them being able to receive voter identification cards, ration cards and drivers license in India.

The reason the Bangladesh-India border cannot be better secured is we have a complicated border where both Bangladesh and India have enclaves inside each other's territories. Unless a proper exchange is done—the agreement that has been worked out means that India loses virtually no land in the process—these enclaves will remain a no man's lands and a safe haven for all kinds of arms smugglers and terrorists.

But unless the Indian Parliament passes this, the border will remain a critical worry for India. Who will settle the border issues, who can?

13. What They Want

Guess which has been one of the most prominent voices in demanding more economic reforms in India? It is some of the most erudite leaders of the dalit community.

Why?

It is encapsulated in a line that researcher and scholar Chandra Bhan Prasad has made famous, 'Pizza delivery ka koi jaath nahin hota.'

When I started writing this book, I went to meet Prasad, who is also the mentor of DICCI (Dalit Indian Chamber of Commerce and Industry), the business council of dalit entrepreneurs which has 3,000 members. Now you might ask, if economics was changing everything about the caste divide, why we would need a separate chamber of commerce for dalits? Why can't dalit entrepreneurs, for instance, be part of FICCI (Federation of Indian Chambers of Commerce and Industry) or CII (Confederation of Indian Industry) or ASSOCHAM (Associated Chambers of Commerce and Industry in India) instead of DICCI?

Well, because things don't change quite so swiftly in India after all. For

Pizza delivery ka koi jaath nahin hota

instance, Prasad brought up cases where dalit entrepreneurs provided critical service to very large Indian manufacturing companies—from the Tatas to Bajaj—but wouldn't tell me their names. Why is that? 'Because they have only recently entered the system within the last few years and revealing their identity might just do more harm than good,' he said.

Basically prejudice takes a long time to be erased. It is better to let these fledgling business-people really grow and form wings before they name themselves and face confidently any bias that comes their way. Remember we are dealing here with prejudice—often violent prejudice—that goes back hundreds of years.

That does not mean no dalit entrepreneur is coming out. From agriculturists to logistics companies to pipe makers, enterprise in the dalit community has received a never-before prominence.

Based on his research on how economics and prosperity transform caste equations—'a satellite TV becomes a more powerful social marker than the sacred thread of the Brahmin'—Prasad coined a new slogan when the debate on foreign direct investment (FDI) in retail was happening in India.

He said: 'FDI lao, Manu bhagao.'

Now whether you agree with him or not on the impact of FDI in retail to the Indian economy, his fundamental logic of change is impossible to deny. It goes like this. When Chandra Bhan Prasad thinks about FDI in retail, he thinks of the mandi system.

Now the mandi system through which all food, fruits, vegetables and grain in India passes through, is dominated by adhatiyas who are an upper caste clan who dominate all mandis across India and have done so for as long as anyone can remember.

There is, and never has been, a dalit adhatiya.

Prasad said he studied how opportunity and success happens for dalits with the University of Pennsylvania's Centre for Advanced Study of India. They found one common thing—Dalits succeed best in non-traditional, non-localised environments. Tradition and local culture holds back the dalit. It is in the new professions, in cities far away from their segregated habitats of small towns and villages, that the dalit is truly free to discover his or her maximum potential. Call centre ka, as it were, koi jaath nahin hota.

Prasad admires Rahul Gandhi for being the one politician who has constantly brought the dalit issue to the forefront of his politics but he says many dalits are shrugging off government moves like the Food Security Act and the Mahatma Gandhi National Rural Employment Guarantee Act, popularly called MNREGA.

'There are villages after villages in Uttar Pradesh where I have seen that dalits point to a house and say, woh toh MNREGA wala ghar hai. There is no pride in being a MNREGA family. It means that you have not made it and have to survive on handouts from the government.'

He says many dalits, especially if they are not very elderly, today view government schemes like the MNREGA as a ploy to keep them in the villages—where they are eternally trapped in many cases in the vile caste system—and not migrate. According to Prasad, migration to the city or the town, economic growth and success, anonymity, new professions—these are shattering caste prejudices more than any government scheme ever could.

Now you could argue here that perhaps only the relatively more prosperous dalits can make this argument and the extremely poor are just grateful for whatever they get but there is powerful thought in Prasad's argument. Do these arguments shatter old, popular government myths?

14. You, Yes You. How Much Do You Care About the Poor?

I think of it as trying to understand the 'roll-up the windows' syndrome. You know what I mean, don't you? It's that moment when the grubby fingers of that filthy, smiling child is reaching out towards the window pane of your car, and you, quick fingered, nimble, non-somnolent, zip up the window pane just in time. It is that moment.

A couple of years ago, the open government foundation I am part of, called the Whypoll Trust, did a research report with the United Nations Millennium Campaign and CVOTER (Centre for Voting Opinion & Trends in Election Research). It tried to understand, one of the first times through research, if not the first time, in India, what the middle class, the relatively rich India really thinks about their poorer brethren.

If you look at what we found, and read between the lines, you will see all our collective hypocrisy about the poor pour out. You will see hints and glimpses of myriad government policies play out, you will see why we decide the kind of so-called poverty alleviation policies that we decide, and why they sometimes succeed, and other times fail.

What we found—after writing series of questions and running them by 5,000 respondents across 38 cities—Mumbai, Surat, Patna, Nasik, Asansol, Raipur, Delhi, Pune, Bhopal, Ghaziabad, Srinagar, Kochi, Chennai, Kanpur, Ludhiana, Meerut, Guwahati, Jammu, Kolkata, Jaipur, Thane, Varanasi, Maisuru, Ahmedabad, Lucknow, Agra, Amritsar, Vijayawada, Banglore, Nagpur, Vadodara, Allahabad, Bhubaneswar, Hyderabad, Indore, Faridabad,Visakhapatnam, Thiruvananthapuram—was this:

- Who are the poor? 27 per cent said the homeless, you know, the people we see wandering around. 24 per cent said hungry children, and 22 per cent said beggars on the streets.
- 41 per cent said poverty is a big problem, and actually it can be solved easily. While 39.2 per cent said it's a big problem, and we won't be able to solve it easily.
- Can we do something about it? 33 per cent said, yes, we can, but 28.3 per cent said, sorry, there's nothing for us to do.
- If we were to do something about it, what would be do? 20 per cent said let's give money to non-governmental organisations (NGOs). Donating money to educational institutions came a close second (17 per cent) whereas helping beggars and homeless (15.3 per cent) and donating money to religious institutions (14.3 per cent) came next in the line of responses.
- But what do we really know about how much poverty there is in India? Our respondents were not sure. 60 per cent thought 30 per cent to 50 per cent of all Indians were poor. Most of them had no clue about where they got their information about poverty from but a third said poverty was underestimated and 71.9 per cent said that the government should spend more on poverty.

- But spend on what? More than six out of ten feel that the government should distribute free food.

And finally the most curious response.

- Half of the total respondents said the middle class Indian does not care about poverty. And 62.7 per cent said specifically the rich don't care. But 61 per cent said the middle class shouldn't be taxed more to help pay for more anti-poverty measures. So who will pay for this? 64 per cent said that the rich should.

It was one of the most fascinating exercises we have ever done at Whypoll and if you think about it, it all adds up. Polls are fought in India in the name of the poor. But the people who can actually do something for the poor have, at best, a fractured and hazy knowledge about who the poor are and what they need. And mostly their response is—let the government do something, anything, and let the rich pay for it. Who are these rich people who will pay for it? Well, anyone who is richer than the person answering the question it seems! It is an apathy that plagues you and me. And while the emergence of a from-the-people and by-the-people political party in the Aam Aadmi Party (AAP) is one great way to engage, our engagement has to show every day, in millions of tiny civic behaviours. Sadly, it does not.

The people who can actually do something for the poor have at best, a fractured and hazy knowledge about who the poor are and what they need

15. Ma, Behen and the City

When night falls among the SUVs, slipping below the asphalt of some of India's best built streets, in this country where smooth roads still have the power to astonish and delight, the crows pretend to be bats.

Fear, shushing and occasionally full of braggadocio in the sunlight, stretches its well-gymnasium-ed lumps, airing the unshaved under-arms, and adding beer to breath, steps out recklessly.

As it grows, so it growls.

Seven empires, they say, are buried beneath Delhi, perhaps eight. Who knows for certain? The latest has been the hungriest, eating up villages and turning them into acronyms. The National Capital Region, NCR, fat cat letters all, they could stand for Never Caught Restrained. Ever yawning across Gurgaon, Ghaziabad, Noida and Faridabad, the satellite towns of aspiration of middle class India, added to Delhi form the NCR. But in millions of minds, the name is Delhi. Dilli, we who live here call it, the city of power and possibility. I prefer to think of it as a sort of Greater Delhi in a place where the naturally OTT population loves naming things greater—Greater Kailash, Greater Noida, what have you.

The tale of the Indian National Capital Region or Greater Delhi is the tale of India; a story where so many things have changed in the last 20 liberalising years, even more so in the last decade.

But the nature of all change, as we know in India, is archaeological. When the shades thrust, new realities crumble out.

Up until the turn of the millennium, almost a decade after Manmohan Singh, then finance minister (and now prime minister), had quoted Victor Hugo and said no power on earth could stop India from letting lose millions (billions?) of entrepreneurs from the old state license shackles. India's capital was smoke city, full of homicidal bus drivers, and dirty buses puking diesel fumes, with newspapers screaming blood on the streets.

Curiously, there was a capitalistic twist to the tale. In 1992, barely a year after the no-power-on-earth-ing, Jagdish Tytler, then surface transport minister, faced with striking drivers of the government-owned Delhi Transport Corporation, adopted the Singh euphemism—he 'opened up' the sector.

Within days, around 4,000 public bus operators mushroomed. Where did they come from? How were they trained? Who were they? No one knew but by the end of the decade, these Red Line and Blue Line buses had become killing machines.

Death on its mean streets has, at least for the last two decades, been the best metaphor for deadly Delhi. Each city needs a space for its sins, the playing field of its Mr. Hyde. Mumbai has its slums, London, the tube, New York, its Hell's Kitchen, and Rio its favelas. In Delhi, it's the roads. Every foul psychology in this city of princes and power, is played out on its streets.

At the turn of the millennium came a benign grandmotherly chief minister. Sheila Dikshit planted trees, broke the back of the transport unions and forced buses and the thieving three-wheel autorickshaws to switch to CNG from diesel and brought in the swishing metro rail. All this won her three elections.

But the streets, they have remained mean. Under her benign gaze, Delhi bagged an epithet, the Rape Capital of India. It consistently tops charts of the worst crime rates against women among 35 Indian mega cities with more than a million people.

Ask Dikshit, as I did in 2009 when the city-state went to polls (just before her hat-trick), and she, correctly, pointed out that when people say Delhi these days, they don't mean Delhi. They mean NCR. In Gurgaon, the Haryana state government is in charge. Noida and Ghaziabad are ruled by Uttar Pradesh. Even in Delhi, police is controlled by the federal Home Ministry.

She has never said this explicitly but there was a hope that as Dikshit modernized the city, India's capital would become more sanitized, even civil. After all, the average person living in Delhi earns around three times the national per capita income today, an additional feather in the cap of the chief minister who also doubles as Delhi's finance minister.

But Dikshit remained defeated on the streets. (And thus was defeated even in the polls in 2013, losing even her own seat to Arvind Kejriwal of the Aam Aadmi Party).

Delhi, the Rape Capital of India, consistently tops charts of the worst crime rates against women among 35 Indian mega cities with more than a million people

The buses are clean, often air-conditioned, but the men, as they will tell you in Delhi, still drive the cars like they treat the women. They stomp, they bruise, they thrust on the accelerator like drunken rapists.

As they drive, so they prey.

The vehicles, though, are different.

A lady friend wrote the other day on Facebook, 'Luxury car ownership should also require a license like a gun license—Mercedes, BMW, Lamborghini all becoming the weapons on Delhi roads!'

'Come on, yaar,' a man immediately replied, 'these are machines with brute raw power, and the thrill of driving them is like riding and taming a wild stallion.'

With every notch of prosperity, Delhi has found new ways to nefariousness. Look at malls—once the glittering towers of a modern city, today many of these are feared for their dimly lit and isolated parking lots. In the forthcoming municipal polls of Delhi, when one sitting councillor has already allegedly murdered a competitor, some activists have been demanding women parking attendants after dark.

In Gurgaon, a skyline of borrowed names ('Kensington Park', 'Central Park', 'Richmond Estate') and aspirations have been fuelled on easy money.

Gurgaon—like much of NCR—is the badlands of the bored landlord, a city of the vacuous and recent-landowner. This has transformed Greater Delhi into a land of idle men. Men who have nothing to do and have the money to do nothing—or men who are, ostensibly, looking for work and have nothing to do, and can, for some time, afford to do nothing. The mind of the idle man, as a senior Delhi policeman recently reminded me, is the devil's workshop.

With a booming economy, two things have happened in the last twenty years. First, Mumbai became one of the most expensive real estates in the world, unaffordable not just for the new, or upcoming entrepreneur, but for many large companies, including the bump-and-ride new BPOs or technology outsourcing companies of India. So they came to Delhi, to be closer to the powers that be and bask in a lovely winter.

But high rises are prohibited inside Delhi, so they snaked up in Gurgaon and Noida. For every new office, one villager became rich, remained little educated and socially primitive, and got cash to burn the night away.

So it is in Gurgaon that they licensed a 'wine shop' every few hundred metres. So it is in Gurgaon that private security guards outnumber police by three times. In the liberalized world, cities were up for sale and someone forgot to inform the sleeping authorities that the citizen cannot always buy safety.

As it grows, so it grimaces. India's National Capital Region is at war. As in so many other parts of India, the side that is winning is the side with money and muscle power.

As Mumbai is ever so often described as a failed city in a failed state, with roads, water and air beyond repair, Delhi wants to grab Mumbai's old crown of cosmopolitanism.

On one side, more people from around the world, and indeed India, are pouring into Delhi and its satellite towns every day, drawn by the spotlights of its growth; but on the other, the barbaric Delhi is hitting back as new money behind new wheels molests, or mows down, at will.

The National Capital Region needs furious citizen activism, participation and contesting in local elections and accountability for elected representatives.

It needs high tech information sharing between police across three states. According to Delhi police, it takes at an average 20 minutes to commit a crime and flee the geographic borders of Delhi and melt into the villages of Haryana or Uttar Pradesh. Delhi NCR has become a sieve of ever shifting crime and criminals.

In 2011, when the Whypoll Trust mapped the first 100 most unsafe places in Delhi, our biggest find in the survey was that almost everyone surveyed began by saying 'everywhere' is unsafe in India's capital. India's capital needs better safety mapping, well-lit toilets for women, powerful lights in parking lots and exemplary punishment to crime, especially against women.

The National Crime Records Bureau numbers show that between the years 2007 and 2011, Delhi had the highest number of reported cases of rape among Indian cities. In 2011, Delhi had 568 cases of reported rape, while Mumbai had 218. It is a city full of illegal transportation of every shape and form—from illegal private buses to illegal modified scooters turned into vans called Gramin Sewa to illegal taxis.

In Gurgaon in September 2013, armed gangs beat up an auto driver and told the two young women travelling into the autorickshaw, 'We will not rape you like they did in the Delhi gang rape case, but if you agree we will let you off later.' This happened barely days after the death sentences were delivered in the Jyoti Singh Pandey case.

It is a city that needs to be reminded, each of us need to be reminded, that in spite of the gang rape and murder of Jyoti Singh Pandey and the protests that followed, in spite of the death sentences to most of her killers, the lawyer of the convicted murderers said, after the sentencing, that if his daughter was out in the night with her boyfriend like Pandey was, he would have burnt her alive. As this book was going to press, the gruesome rape of a Danish tourist in Delhi told us again that nothing was changing.

Or it needs Batman. As Bruce Wayne is told in *The Dark Knight Rises* there is a storm coming. And the storm is coming, where is our defence?

16. 11 Reasons to Worry For India

Reason 1

Only 16 countries, outside Africa, had a lower gross national per capita than India in 2010.

Reason 2

Life expectancy at birth in India is now three years shorter than in Bangladesh.

Reason 3

Child mortality is 24 per cent lower in Bangladesh than in India.

Reason 4

Social indicators of Nepal and India are nearly the same today, though per capita income of India is three times that of Nepal.

Reason 5

In every count, adjusted to every metric, China spends much more on public health than India.

Reason 6

At the poverty line income of around Rs 30, in Delhi, a person can get 1 kg rice and a bus ride for three stops.

Reason 7

The proportion of women in the Lok Sabha has never risen beyond 10 per cent.

Reason 8

Only 5 countries, outside Africa, have lower youth female literacy rate than India.

Reason 9

Only 4 countries fare worse than India in child mortality (Afghanistan, Haiti, Myanmar, Cambodia and Pakistan).

Reason 10

Only 3 countries have lower levels of access to sanitation (Bolivia, Cambodia and Haiti) than India.

Reason 11

No country, not even Africa, has a higher number of underweight children.

Ashamed yet?

17. D for...?

For those who are empire-philes, there has been an authentic touch of the old colonial world recently, full of the old romance of the high tea, bearers, howdahs and palanquins. One of the British Raj's old beloved diseases, dengue caused by the bite of the female Aedes aegypti mosquito, was back with a vengeance.

You may have missed it, what with all the electioneering and 100 crore Bollywood films filling the news, but India has been going through a dengue epidemic.

I know at least 10 people who got it. As one journalist pointed out, everyone knows several people who got it, and/or, they got it themselves.

There is a small thing about dengue. People actually die from it.

You may ask why you need to be given this trivia before an election. I cite two simple reasons:

A. It showed how ill-prepared even the Indian capital was, to deal with what is basically a non-fatal disease (unless neglected—say for instance if there are not enough hospital beds in the capital of the world's we-are-about-to-get-there superpower to deal with the patients—and then it kills swiftly. How do I know this? Well, I knew someone who died in one week).

Delhi alone reported around 4,600 cases of Dengue

B. And it showed the extent of under-reporting of the disease by government agencies. The latest government figures before this book went to press was 109 dead and 38,179 cases in all (double the number of previous years). Delhi alone reported around 4,600 cases but doctors have been saying that, after a point they just stopped counting and the director of the National Vector Borne Disease Control Programme told the BBC that it was 'very, very difficult to get accurate numbers'.

Moral of the story? Government numbers are sometimes suspect, and there are leftover stuff from the Raj we still haven't been able to get rid of. Saying 'ayes' and 'nay'-es during voice votes in Parliament—even though no one says aye and nay in daily life in India—is not the only relic we are clinging on to. There's also dengue.

18. The 'Not Hidden, Not Terrorist'

Hafiz Saeed, accused of masterminding the 26/11 terror attacks in Mumbai and being the founding father of the Lashkar-e-Taiba, the group responsible for some of the most deadly attacks in Kashmir, lives and preaches in Pakistan. (He denies that he had anything to do with 26/11 or the Lashkar.)

The core content of everything he says is always the same: India is evil. India wants to ruin Pakistan. India has no right over Kashmir. Kashmir must be 'freed' at any cost. (He does not deny any of these statements and is happy to repeat them any time you want.)

Unlike Dawood Ibrahim, Hafiz Saeed, who has a $10 million (around Rs 62 crore) US bounty on his head, is not someone whose address/es are suspect. He is not hiding like Osama bin Laden.

Saeed accuses India of damming rivers that go to that country, of causing unrest and terror attacks in Balochistan, of trying to stop the funding of his charitable organisation Jamaat-ud-Dawa (which most security reports say is a front for the Lashkar-e-Taiba). He has been arrested thrice in Pakistan and then let off by the courts for lack of evidence. Jamaat-ud-Dawa is considered, by India, America, Britain, the European Union, Russia and Australia, to be a terrorist organisation.

He has said that he will not rest until Kashmir is 'freed'.

He has said India can never take strong military action against Pakistan because Pakistan's 'atom bombs are not for the museum'.

Reports suggest that he lives in Lahore. He lives in a villa, which also has an adjoining mosque and office. He has police protection. He was banned from entering Islamabad, it is said, but his latest rally—where his supporters pledged to unleash 'many Mumbai-s' on India—was in Islamabad. Thousands attended the rally and called for jihad against India.

In the last few years, Hafiz Saeed has emerged as one of the most vocal voices against India and indeed India's security threat is a key election point and it is important to understand the people who cause this threat.

Not much information about Hafiz Saeed is available but most of the information on him comes from an interview he gave to an Urdu language newspaper, *Roznama Ummat*, in Karachi in 2012.

According to that interview, he was born in Faisalabad in Pakistan and raised in Sargodha in the Pakistan side of Punjab. (Though there is also an Arundhati Roy piece in the *Guardian* which suggests that he was from Shimla, and it is not clear why Roy thinks so.)

In the interview, Saeed says he was born in 1950 and since his childhood he had heard stories of 36 members of his family being killed in the violence during the partition

Hafiz Saeed has said India can never take strong military action against Pakistan because Pakistan's 'atom bombs are not for the museum'

of India and Pakistan as his father and his extended family made their way from Haryana to across the border, a journey he says took four months.

Saeed grew up in a small village and has two postgraduate degrees in Arabic and Islamic Studies. He was a lecturer at the University of Engineering and Technology in Lahore when, in 1981, he got a scholarship to study in the King Saud University in Riyadh. There Saeed worked under the tutelage of Sheikh Abdul Aziz bin Baz—whose most famous student was Osama bin Laden.

Now this naturally does not mean Saeed is another Osama bin Laden; it is merely a fact that he mentioned in this interview. From Baz, Saeed got the inspiration of starting the Jamaat-ud-Dawa, which has done exemplary social work in Pakistan, especially during calamities, but is widely considered to be the front for the Lashkar-e-Taiba.

During his time as president of Pakistan, Pervez Musharraf banned the Jamaat-ud-Dawa, arresting Saeed several times.

Today Saeed promises that the goal of his life is a 'free Kashmir'. He is said to have defined his career by wanting to bleed India with a thousand cuts, which echoes what Indian defence analysts have been saying about the long time strategic aim of the Pakistan Army in supporting militancy in India,

We vote also to keep ourselves safe. It is worth thinking who among the parties contesting the elections has any relevant strategy to engage and neutralise the threat from Hafiz Saeed and men like him.

19. The Man Who is Not Scared of the Naxals

The Indian politician fears the Naxal. This is particularly true after the attack on 25 May 2013 when rebels killed 27 people in a convoy of Congress politicians in the Darbha Valley of the Sukma district of Chhattisgarh. Among the dead was the state Congress chief, Nand Kumar Patel and Mahendra Karma, former state chief and the infamous father of the anti-Naxal private armies, Salwa Judum. Later, the old warhorse of the Congress, Vidya Charan Shukla, died of his injuries.

Some politicians have tried to reach out to the rebels—Bengal Chief Minister, Mamata Banerjee, for instance before she won the elections in her state—but such efforts have quickly soured. Now Banerjee says that the Maoists want to kill her, and sees Maoists everywhere, even in school girls asking questions.

But there is one man who is different. And his example bears thinking about when we decide what kind of politicians can deal with what is one of India's greatest security threats, Maoist violence.

I wanted to write about Tribal Affairs and Panchayati Raj Minister, Vyricherla Kishore Chandra Suryanarayana Deo, after Ravi Rebbapragada, a forest rights activist, told me that Deo was different from other politicians because he entered the forests without fear. And where are these forests? These are the forests of Visakhapatnam in coastal Andhra Pradesh. Deo's own constituency, the sylvan Araku Valley, is one of the largest parliamentary areas in the country at more than 3,500 square kilometres, and it is also one of the most pristine forest areas in the country.

But these forests are also the nerve centre of Maoist activity in the region. Visakhapatnam was the area where 11 government officers were kidnapped by rebels in 1987; in 1993, Pasupuleti Balaraju, then a Member of the Legislative Assembly and now state tribal affairs minister, was kidnapped and later exchanged for the release of a top rebel, and in March 2004, the husband of then tribal affairs minister Mani Kumari, was shot dead by a member of the Peoples War Group (one of the many militant groups that later formed the Communist Party of India [Maoist]).

Rebbapragada told me that Deo's clout with the locals, whether Maoists or not, can be seen every time the minister visits his constituency. 'He travels with barely one constable, if that. Compare that with when the state tribal affairs minister, Balaraju, comes to the area; there is always a huge convoy, there is security everywhere, the routes are checked for mines; it becomes a jamboree.'

Why is this true? Because Deo stands alone in blocking a group of large and influential mining companies, which want to mine these forests for bauxite, used to make aluminium. Beneath the woods of these forests lie more than 42 million tonnes of bauxite: throw in the neighbouring areas, and there are more than 570 million tonnes of the mineral waiting to be tapped.

'I have seen the timber mafia cut down forests and then burn even the stumps so that they can accuse the tribals of slash and burn agriculture. These are the kind of atrocities that have gone on for decades,' Deo told me. 'The main cause is lack of development and destruction of forests by the timber mafia. If the Maoist problem is only seen as a law and order problem, then that is completely flawed.'

He refused to elaborate on the 'timber mafia' but last year, in a report presented to Congress president, Sonia Gandhi, Deo allegedly referred to the head of the Congress committee in Andhra Pradesh, Botsa Satyanarayana, as a 'don' with interests in 'liquor, land and mining'.

There is a bit of history in all this. In the 1990s, a Supreme Court judgment ruled that no land in tribal areas can be leased to private mining companies and that village *gram sabhas* or councils would have the right to prevent such exploration. The court added that minerals can be extracted only by tribals historically living in the area either individually or through a cooperative society with the financial assistance of the state, and at least 20 per cent of the profits must go into a permanent fund for the development of the locals. It also prohibited any transfer of any lease or fresh lease of land to any non-tribal.

The Andhra Pradesh government signed agreements with mining giants from around the world through APMDC, claiming that the corporation was a 'local' company. 'But that was fundamentally wrong,' Rebbapragada told me. 'The APMDC was basically just signing the deed while all the work would be done by the private companies and the real power on the ground was with private companies who had nothing to do with tribals.'

If the Maoist problem is only seen as a law and order problem, then that is completely flawed

Deo has prevented a Rs 25,000 crore exploration of the region by major companies, including the Ras Al Khaimah government of the United Arab Emirates, its Indian partner Anrak—a subsidiary of Hyderabad-based Penna Cement, Jindal South West of the JSW Group and Nalco, the state-run aluminium major. Three of these—Ras Al Khaimah, Anraka, and Jindal South West—have signed agreements with the Andhra Pradesh Mineral Development Corporation (APMDC) to mine in this region. (As a government body, Nalco has not signed an agreement, but was awarded mines here in an auction.)

Deo says he's merely enforcing what's already there in the constitution. Under the Alienation of Land Transfer Act, non-tribals in Schedule 5 areas are strictly prohibited from buying or leasing land. The Indian Constitution defines Schedule 5 and 6 as regions historically inhabited by tribals who live in and off the forest lands. In Schedule 6 areas—the north-eastern states—the tribal populations are a majority, whereas in Schedule 5 areas—Andhra Pradesh, Odisha, Jharkhand and Chhattisgarh—tribals are numerous, though not a majority.

In a 14-page letter to the governor of Andhra Pradesh, Ekkadu Srinivasan Lakshminarasimhan, in April 2013, Deo hit out against one of Andhra Pradesh's most popular Congress chief ministers, Y.S. Rajasekhara Reddy, popularly called YSR, who died in a helicopter crash in 2009. In his letter, Deo criticises the agreements signed between APMDC and various mining companies between 2005 and 2011, claiming that the 'local' company was 'neither owned nor controlled by people belonging to Scheduled Tribes'. This, he says, is a betrayal of the tribals and 'amounts to a flagrant violation and affront of our constitutional provisions.'

To understand the reasons behind this criticism, a little history may help. Like Deo, YSR was a veteran Congress hand,

and for 30 years had won every election he had contested. When he came to power as chief minister in 2004, India was fast becoming the world's third largest exporter of bauxite, shipping half of its annual nearly 100 million tonnes of output to a growing China. 'YSR could see that potentially, minerals could bring in much more money than information technology (the previous chief minister, N. Chandrababu Naidu, focussed on IT to international acclaim), especially in the short run,' says an MP from Andhra Pradesh who asked not to be named.

In July 2005, YSR's government signed the first Memorandum of Understanding (MoU) with Jindal South West. According to the agreement, the Jindals would spend Rs 9,000 crore to create an aluminium refinery and smelter which would produce 250,000 tonnes of aluminium each year. APMDC was to supply the bauxite from the Araku reserves and its neighbouring Sapparla reserves, which together had more than 240 million tonnes of ore. Then, in 2007 and 2008, APMDC signed similar MoUs with the government of Ras Al Khaimah and Anrak, respectively. (Anrak is a joint venture between the Ras Al Khaimah government and Penna Cements, owned by Prathap Reddy, YSR's friend.)

In each case, the Maoists fought fiercely to protect the forests from miners and violence in the region went up. Deo, then not a minister, was convinced that mining in the Araku and Sapparla areas would result in a bloody backlash, and said so on several occasions. For YSR, however, the only answer to militants was gunfire, and he sent elite Greyhound commandos into the forest to attack Maoist camps and kill rebel leaders. His hard line was widely hailed by politicians and businesspeople.

There is also another ideological difference.

Deo has no commercial interests and no income from any source apart from agricultural monies from his family lands. 'I am a farmer, have always been one,' says the minister. In comparison, YSR's empire, now managed by his son Jaganmohan Reddy, sprawled across 13 companies, from TV stations to power stations and cement. When Reddy, now in prison in a disproportionate assets case, contested a by-poll in 2011 after his father's death, he declared assets of Rs 365 crore. The Central Bureau of Investigation says that's only the tip of the iceberg.

With YSR gone, Deo's voice against destructive mining grew ever stronger.

In the letter to the Andhra governor, Deo wrote: 'During the last five years, they [the Maoist rebels] have slowly regrouped themselves by gaining the sympathy of the local people only due to the threat of bauxite mining in Visakhapatnam district.' Most of the killings, he added, were 'in connection with those who are said to have had close links with the bauxite mining lobbies and their agents.'

He also denounced the YSR-era mining agreements, saying 'the mala fide intentions are abundantly clear', referring to the fact that the Anrak MoU was signed by Y. Srilakshmi, the former (state) secretary of industry and commerce who is now in prison in the Obulapuram illegal mining case. Former APMDC MD P.D. Rajagopal who signed the supply agreement between APMDC and Anrak is also in jail (in the same case).

Deo sent similar letters to the governors of other states suffering from Maoist violence: Jharkhand, Chhattisgarh and Odisha.

Deo says he's not an obstructionist who is in the way of economic development. All he is trying to do is to ensure that tribals have a voice in the development of their localities. 'I go by empirical evidence. I am not against mining but I have seen that in region after region, indiscriminate mining has brought no benefits to the people.' Indeed, he argues, like many others, that winning over the tribals is the best way to fight the Maoists.

Deo's work raises a vital question we really ought to be discussing as a key issue before the elections—but as usual are not—is our strategy of engaging tribal populations largely flawed? Where are we going wrong? And how can we correct it?

20. 5 Scams You Must Remember Before Voting

1. 2G Spectrum Telecom Scam

The Comptroller and Auditor General of India (CAG) said the scam of undervaluing telecom spectrum was worth Rs 176,000 crore. The Central Bureau of Investigation said a more modest Rs 30,000 crore.

One cabinet minister, Andimuthu Raja of the Dravida Munnetra Kazhagam, went to prison. He is now out on bail.

2. Coal Block Allotment Scam

The CAG calculated that 'the financial impact of the benefit to the private allottees' in this scam, on allotment of coal blocks to be mined, was Rs 185,591 crore.

One Congress leader and industrialist, Naveen Jindal, has been questioned in this scandal. Pushed to a corner, the former coal secretary has pointed fingers at the prime minister. Famously many files in this case were missing, at one point up to 200 of them!

3. The Helicopter Scam

A Rs 3,600 crore deal was made with AgustaWestland and its parent company, Finmeccanica, for the supply of 12 helicopters. A number of military officials and politicians were accused of accepting bribes from AgustaWestland when the deal came to light.

Former air chief marshal Shashi Tyagi became the first air service chief to be accused in a scandal. Other accused included a brother of former union minister Santosh Bagrodia, called Satish Bagrodia. After intensive media attention on the scam, the Indian government was forced to cancel the deal.

4. Commonwealth Games Scam

The loss might have been only Rs 90 crore (a pittance compared to the other scandals) but this was arguably one of India's biggest international embarrassments.

A team led by Congress politician, Suresh Kalmadi, who was later accused of graft and imprisoned, made a mess of the preparations of the 2010 Commonwealth Games in Delhi.

As the world sniggered, reports emerged of contracts being given to dubious firms, even though there were cheaper bids. Rolls of toilet paper went for $80 a roll, soap dispensers for $61 and first-aid kits for $125.

5. Uttar Pradesh NRHM Scam

The Mayawati government in Uttar Pradesh is accused of having stolen 5,000 crore of funds from the National Rural Health Mission.

How likely is the party of the candidate you are voting for to steal from the country once they are in power?

This is apart from the mysterious murders of at least six men associated with medical supplies in the state, including two chief medical officers of the state and two deputy chief medical officers—one of them only one day before he was to make a critical appearance in court.

At least two ministers of the former Mayawati government are accused in this scam, one of who happily shifted parties just before the elections and joined the Bharatiya Janata Party (BJP).

How likely is the party of the candidate you are voting for to steal from the country, from you and me, once they are in power?

21. Debt Do Us Part

'What worries me deeply,' economist and Labour peer Meghnad Desai told me, 'even before a big poll, no leading politician is willing to discuss critical economic issues.'

What is he talking about?

Fiscal responsibility, spending far more than you earn, debt, repayment and inflation.

'When you pay a third of revenues towards interest payments, there's less money for everything else, including building critical infrastructure.'

India's current account which had a surplus of $14 billion in 2003-04, now has a deficit of close to $90 billion or nearly 5 per cent of GDP. A sustainable level would be around half of that. (Finance Minister P. Chidambaram has said that he will defy naysayers and keep the current account deficit, CAD, to under $70 billion in the fiscal year ending March 2014.)

Also by 31 March 2014, India has to pay back $172 billion in short-term debt maturing within a year. In March 2008, the amount was $54.7 billion. In this period the current account deficit grew from about 2.5 per cent in 2008–09 to nearly 5 per cent in 2012–13. Short-term debt maturing within a year is now almost 60 per cent of India's total foreign exchange reserves. In March 2008, it was 17 per cent. The rupee's downward slide against the dollar hasn't helped.

'The worry is that even though the finance minister might talk about these issues from time to time, there is really no larger debate that unless fiscal responsibility is very high on our agenda, we cannot forever live beyond our means,' said Desai.

And it is not just the government that is indebted. Look at what is happening to India Inc. As my colleague at *Fortune India*, Ashish Gupta, pointed out in October 2013, many Indian banks 'may have just received the knockout punch'. He reported that State Bank of India, the largest public sector bank, had gross non-performing assets (NPAs, or money lent that is unlikely to come back) of Rs 13,766 crore in the first quarter of financial year 2014, up from Rs 5,868 crore in the fourth quarter of 2013. Gross NPAs of 40 listed Indian banks went up by 43 per cent in one year.

Gupta quoted a Credit Suisse report House of Debt, to say that the total debt of 10 infrastructure companies accounts for 98 per cent of the net worth of all banks and said that if these companies go down, the lenders are definite to take a huge hit on their balance sheets.

What does this mean for you and me?

Apart from the doomsday scenario—not so remote after all—of banks collapsing under debt, it is worth remembering that the government says that three lakh crore rupees is needed to complete building India's highways. Most of this money is supposed to come from the private sector but if the banks are so cash-deprived, who will do the lending?

Then there is inflation—the third of the big three things that Desai told me keeps him awake at night. 'Sometimes I feel that the Indian government uses inflation as a tool of income redistribution. It's a scandal.'

The week I am writing this, wholesale prices climbed 6.46 per cent compared to the year before and consumer prices rose 9.84 per cent. Essentially it seems like we are paying more for food with each passing week.

Desai also points to what he calls the detrimental impact of government-fixed minimum support price for wheat on food inflation. Food Minister, K.V. Thomas, seemed to agree with Desai when he rejected Agriculture Minister Sharad Pawar's suggestion for a Rs 100 hike from Rs 1,350 to Rs 1,450 on wheat procurement price and settled for Rs 1,400 instead.

And while talking about debt, it makes sense to take a quick peek at the states:

The top five debt laden states are: Maharashtra, Uttar Pradesh, West Bengal, Gujarat and Andhra Pradesh.

Now the point about debt is not so much the money owed but what it is being spent on. The things economists look at are: how much the state is earning, what is the growth amount of tax money coming in and where is the money being spent. Is it being spent on building roads and bridges and hospitals and spaces for business—all of which add to the growth of the state or is it being spent on things like paying salaries to a deeply inefficient bureaucracy?

That's where the difference between states like West Bengal, where most of the money coming in is paid in salaries to a highly inefficient mass of state employees, and the other states lie.

In the meantime, consumer-price inflation climbed to 11.24 per cent last November, the highest among 17 Asia-Pacific counties—according to Bloomberg—and the rupee fell 11 per cent last year.

> **The point about debt is not so much the money owed but what it is being spent on**

It might be worthwhile to ask which leaders are most likely to tackle financial responsibility head-on and curb debt and ask ourselves if that is a strong reason for us to vote for them.

22. Who Let the Rations Out?

Now some of the brunt of rise in food prices could be curbed for the poorest if our public distribution system (PDS) worked. After all, a ration shop, the local unit of the PDS system, is supposed to provide foodstuff at highly subsidised, or low, prices.

Does it? Of course, PDS is the original leaky bucket of Indian public services. I remember a time we used to have a ration card too in Calcutta. And so did the domestic help at our home who usually borrowed our cards to get extra quota of sugar or kerosene, since we didn't use much kerosene. But often, the shop would insist that there were no stocks. This, even a decade ago, used to happen with unfailing regularity.

Well, data seems to show that the all-India numbers are still poor (though better than before). The 'leakage' (that process where the ration shop owner sells things in the black market and tells the poor that there are no supplies) has gone down from 55 per cent to 35 per cent between 2004–05 and 2011–12. Some states, though, have done a remarkable job of plugging leakage almost entirely, like Chhattisgarh and the traditional good-at-PDS states like Tamil Nadu (which has universal PDS benefits) and Himachal Pradesh. Even Bihar, a torturously low performer of the past, brought down leakage (we ought to perhaps stop using this harmless sounding word and just call it theft; calling it leakage is a bit like calling sexual harassment eve teasing) from 65 per cent in 2009–10 to 12 per cent in 2011–12.

Leakage: the process by which the ration shop owner sells things in the black market and tells the poor that there are no supplies

Looking at PDS also gives us one of those uniquely Indian problems. In the state of Gujarat, leakage increased from 45 per cent to 69 per cent between 2009–10 and 2011–12, and an economist from the Indian Institute of Technology-Delhi reported that Gujarat has a very high rate of 'diversion', another way of saying that a lot of it is being stolen.

The Justice Wadhwa Committee constituted a look into PDS corruption and mentioned that state authorities had weeded out more than seven lakh bogus ration cards in 2008-09. It also spoke about Gujarat's innovative e-authentication of delivery system as one of the only ways to better delivery. As always there has been a debate on whether Gujarat gets kudos or credit but the larger point is this—solving delivery issues like these is critical to the future of India.

Perhaps it makes sense to think hard on which leaders, if elected, can solve such protracted, historic issues.

23. Riots to Remember

One of the biggest incidents of communal and racial violence in history happened as India got independence in 1947—Partition. Some estimates suggest up to one million Hindus, Muslims and Sikhs were killed as India and Pakistan were created.

Once again as this election approaches, we debate incessantly; what and who is secular, and indeed, communal. We are the nation that lives its history every day, and is yet, so often, forgetful of our past. It is pertinent then to note our experience of friction. I have left out the number of people dead and injured and their religious affiliations from this list because we hear enough of those who died in racial violence in India. We are only too aware of those murders and their burden on our collective conscience. To me, it was more important to note the chronology than repeat the details of the bloodshed yet again. (Please note that these are the prominent skirmishes. There might be many others which happen every other day, and have been happening for decades, which only get listed in the minds of men. I use the word men deliberately because, in spite of a few cases like Maya Kodnani in Gujarat in 2002, most rioters in the history of riots in India are usually men.)

1953 and 1956	Kota, Rajasthan
1961	Jabalpur, Madhya Pradesh
1964	Rourkela, Calcutta, Jamshedpur, then-Bihar (now Jharkhand) and West Bengal
1967	Hatia, Ranchi, Bihar
1968	Aurangabad, Maharashtra
1968	Karimganj, Assam
1969	Ahmedabad, Gujarat
1970	Bhiwandi, Maharashtra
1970	Jalgaon, Maharashtra
1970	Mahad, Maharashtra
1972	Nonari and Sajni, Uttar Pradesh
1977	Varanasi, Uttar Pradesh
1978	Sambhal, Uttar Pradesh
1978	Aligarh, Uttar Pradesh
1978	Hyderabad, Andhra Pradesh
1979	Jamshedpur, then-Bihar (now Jharkhand)
1980	Moradabad, Uttar Pradesh
1981	Biharsharif, Bihar
1982	Meerut, Uttar Pradesh
1982	Baroda, Gujarat
1983	Malur, Karnataka
1983	Malegaon, Maharashtra
1983	Hazaribagh, Bihar
1983	Hyderabad, Andhra Pradesh
1984	Biwandi, Maharashtra
1984	Delhi
1985	Ahmedabad, Gujarat
1986	Ahmedabad, Gujarat
1987	Meerut, Uttar Pradesh
1989	Indore, Madhya Pradesh
1989	Kota, Rajasthan
1989	Bhadrak, Odisha
1990	Several incidents across Gujarat

1990	Jaipur, Rajasthan
1990	Jodhpur, Rajasthan
1990	Lucknow, Uttar Pradesh
1990	Agra, Uttar Pradesh
1990	Kanpur, Uttar Pradesh
1990	Delhi
1990	Hailakandi, Assam
1990	Beawar, Maharashtra
1989 and 1990	Bhagalpur, Bihar
1990	Patna, Bihar
1990	Indore, Madhya Pradesh
1990	Hasan, Mandya, Madikeri and Mysore, Karnataka
1990	Hyderabad, Andhra Pradesh
1991	Several incidents across Gujarat
1991	Varanasi, Uttar Pradesh
1991	Baroda, Uttar Pradesh
1992	Sitamarhi, Bihar
1992	Surat, Gujarat
1992	Bhopal, Madhya Pradesh
December 1992–January 1993	Mumbai, Maharashtra
1995	Chennai, Tamil Nadu
1995	Chitradurga, Karnataka
1995	Kerala
1995	Rankhandi, Uttar Pradesh
1995	Palmau, Bihar
1995	Hyderabad, Andhra Pradesh
1998	Kanpur, Uttar Pradesh
1998	Ajmer, Rajasthan
1998	Coimbatore, Tamil Nadu
1998	Moradabad, Uttar Pradesh
1998	Hyderabad, Andhra Pradesh
1998	Bardoli and Sanjeli, Gujarat

1998	Nalanda and Mungher, Bihar
1998	Ahwa and Dang districts, Gujarat
1998	Suratkul, Karnataka
1999	Manoharpur, Odisha
1999	Ahmedabad, Gujarat
1999	Harda, Madhya Pradesh
1999	Surat, Gujarat
1999	Aurangabad, Maharashtra
2000	Kolhapur, Karnataka
2001	Kishtwar, Jammu and Kashmir
2001	Nalanda, Bihar
2001	Kanpur, Uttar Pradesh
2001	Beawar, Rajasthan
2001	Chamrajnagar, Mysore, Karnataka
2001	Jamner, Maharashtra
2001	Moradabad, Uttar Pradesh
2001	Amravani, Maharashtra
2001	Ahmedabad, Gujarat
2001	Malegaon, Maharashtra
2002	Ahmedabad, Gujarat
2002	Kaithal, Haryana
2002	Bhiwani, Haryana
2002	Parts of Rajasthan
2002	Sholapur, Maharashtra
2002	Qasim Nagar, Jammu and Kashmir
2003	In pockets of Gujarat
2003	Marad, Kerala
2008	Kandhamal, Odisha
2012	Parts of Assam
2013	Muzaffarnagar, Uttar Pradesh

How do we stop this? Who can stop these? Think of these questions before you cast your vote.

24. There is Something in the Air

The World Health Organisation says that more people get lung cancer due to air pollution than, say, second-hand smoke. Its cancer research arm, the International Agency for Research on Cancer (IARC) said that in 2010, 223,000 people died of lung cancer caused by air pollution.

And guess what? Two Indian cities are in the top ten cities in the world with the highest rate of air pollution. At No. 4 is Ludhiana and at No. 10 is Kanpur. Which are the other countries that have cities in the top 10? Iran, Mongolia, Pakistan and Botswana. Notice, for all its fast growth, no China.

Air pollution is described in terms of microgrammes of particulate matter in every cubic metre of air. At the top of the heap is Ahwaz in Iran with 372. Ludhiana is at 251, as is tribal belt of Quetta in Pakistan. Kanpur has 209.

Delhi is not too far away at 198. Mumbai is at 132 and Bengaluru at 90.

Two Indian cities are in the top ten cities in the world with the highest rate of air pollution

The Chinese city with the maximum amount of air pollution is Lanzhou at 150. Beijing is at 121 and Shanghai at 81. The most polluted European city is Plovdiv in Bulgaria (70). The most polluted American city is Bakersfield at 38—the same level as Paris. London is at 29 and New York at 21.

The World Bank says that air pollution costs India around $30 billion a year. If air pollution was taxed (or organisations that pollute were taxed), says the Bank, it could bring in $59 billion in India. The Bank last year put India at 126 of 132 countries in environmental performance and placed us at 132, or last, in the assessment of the impact of air pollution on the citizens of India.

According to the World Health Organisation, India has the world's highest death rate from respiratory diseases and more people are dying of asthma in our country than anywhere else in the world.

Does India have an air pollution plan? Is it working? Is there any party, any leader who has a plan to curb this pollution? How come we never discuss air pollution in our myriad political speeches? Some people say that an election cannot be fought on such policies—people don't care, they don't understand. Really? We, the voters, prefer to hear about bitching, name calling, Pappu Vs Feku, but not about things that are killing us, is it?

Or is this the reason no party, no leader ever agrees to public debates? Is it because they would actually have to talk about policy?

25. The Matters of Excreta

The Centre for Science and Environment (CSE), India's foremost independent research, is not known to mince words. That's why their critical report on waste management is called *Excreta Does Matter*.

This report says 80 per cent—that's right 80 per cent—of sewage in India is untreated and flows directly into the rivers, polluting the main sources of drinking water.

What does this mean?

It means untreated sewage is directly going into the water that comes back to us as drinking water.

Only 20 per cent of the around 40,000 million litres of sewage produced by Indian cities is treated. The Central Pollution Control Board measured, in 2011, that only 160 of around 8,000 Indian towns had sewage treatment facilities.

80 per cent of sewage in India is untreated and pollutes the main sources of drinking water

CSE called this a 'ticking health time bomb'.

There's more. The Comptroller and Auditor General of India wrote a report called the Water Pollution

Report of 2011-2012. It pointed out that water-borne diseases were probably the biggest killer in India and said that in their research they had found that roughly 80 per cent of sewage from Indian cities goes straight into the rivers and into our drinking water. The CAG had more devastating things to add—only 62 per cent of Delhi's sewage is treated, Bengaluru treated only 10 per cent of its sewage, Patna 29 per cent, Kanpur 38 per cent and Hyderabad 43 per cent. Only Ahmedabad had the sewage treatment facilities to treat all its waste. Remember that water borne disease called dengue? Ever heard of election speeches that promise to raise the number of sewage treatment plants?

26. Poisoned Water

In 2012, the water resources ministry told Parliament that,

- Groundwater in 158 of 639 districts in India had gone saline.
- In 267 districts, groundwater had excess fluoride.
- In 385 districts it had nitrates above permissible limits.
- In 53, there was arsenic in the water.
- High level of iron in water was found in 270 districts.

More than 80 per cent of drinking water in India comes from underground sources. The presence of fluorides, arsenic and other chemicals affects everything, from bones and teeth to the nervous system. Large parts of India are, in fact, drinking poisoned water.

In the next two decades, 60 per cent of all aquifers in India will be in a critical situation of scarcity and contamination, says the World Bank. This will be frightening because India is the largest user of groundwater in the world and uses around 230 cubic kilometres of groundwater every year which is a quarter of the global total.

Large parts of India are drinking poisoned water

More than 60 per cent of irrigated agriculture and 85 per cent of drinking water supply in India comes from groundwater. But 29 per cent of all groundwater blocks are semi-critical, critical or overexploited.

A much needed point in the manifesto?

27. It Never Stops

The open government foundation Whypoll Trust requested Debarshi Dey, Ph.D in statistics from the University of California to look at numbers of crimes against women in 2012.

He looked at data between 1998 and 2011 and here's what he found:

- The rate of crimes against women had gone up by around 74 per cent.
- There is a spike in reported cases from 2004 onwards. This we put to better reporting and not just more number of cases.
- Cases of cruelty by the husband or in-laws were 30 per cent.
- Crimes against women as a proportion to the total number of crimes had increased from 7 per cent to 10 per cent and we found that the rate of increase of crimes against women was higher than the average increase in crime
- The rate of increase in cases of domestic violence is highest at 140 per cent, followed by kidnapping at 117 per cent, rape at 60 per cent and molestation at 40 per cent

We knew this from grim personal experience. When Whypoll first started the women's safety campaign that led to the creation of the women's safety mobile app with the tech company CanvasM, some of the first anonymous emails and calls we got were about domestic violence.

The rate of increase of crimes against women was higher than the average increase in crime

In all the heat and dust of violence against women, our research brought us despair and hope. More cases of violence were being reported than ever and we know now that the maximum violence on women happens inside the home and not outside.

Which political party has ever put violence against women as one of their campaign planks? Half of the electorate are women, so why not?

28. Date After Date After Date

Have you seen the Hindi film, *Damini*? It has Sunny Deol playing a rugged, honest, but largely unsuccessful lawyer who takes on the system through one vital case.

That film had many memorable dialogues. In one, Deol talks about his *dhaie kilo ka haath*. When the two-and-a-half kilogramme arm falls on someone, they don't get up, they go up.

The film's other angst-filled rant on *tarik pe tarik* or a justice system that issues date after date to appear for court hearings for years for a single case, but delivers no justice, has never stopped echoing.

There are more than 30 million cases pending in India, 80 per cent of them in the lower courts. The high courts has four million pending cases and the Supreme Court had more than 66,000 cases. The National Court Management System says at the moment there are 19,000 judges—of these 18,000 judges are in trial courts—and sometimes a civil case

The high courts have four million pending cases and the Supreme Court has more than 66,000 cases

can last for 15 years. In the last 30 years, the number of judges had grown six times but the number of cases grew 12 times!

In the next 30 years, India will need 75,000 judges because it will have around 150 million cases. No one really knows where they are going to come from, and no one is really clear about who has a plan to solve this.

29. Our Nearly Unparalleled Corruption

In 2013, India ranked 94 among 176 countries in the Transparency International's Corruption Perception Index. This was the same rank that we had in 2012.

In 2012, just when we were beginning to feel happy that we had improved by one place (in 2011, we were 95), Transparency International said that they had changed the methodology of ranking in 2012 and the ranking could not be compared to 2011.

Thanks.

In 2007, India was ranked 72 among180 countries. After that, we have steadily fallen—as our scams have risen—and in 2010, we were 87.

Let's not embarrass ourselves by mentioning the countries ranked above us but the countries below us were Pakistan, Southern Sudan, Bangladesh, Myanmar, North Korea, Somalia and Nepal among others.

Maybe the problem is with Transparency International?

How do we fare in other rankings then? Let's take the World

Audit Corruption ranking of 2012. India is at 74, below Malawi, Zambia, Burkina Faso and Liberia among others.

Any silver lining?

Yes, in 2013, Transparency International said that among companies in the BRICS nations (Brazil, Russia, India, China and South Africa), Indian companies were most transparent.

So what should our politicians push for: more state-run companies or greater private ownership, especially in non-critical areas?

30. The Suicide-Prone Farmer

The National Crime Record Bureau says around 270,940 farmers have killed themselves in India since 1995. Between 1995 and 2000, they killed themselves at the rate of 14,462 per year and at the rate of 16,743 per year, between 2001 and 2011.

As P. Sainath of the *Hindu* calculated—or as you could if you cared enough—that's around 46 a day, or roughly about one every half hour since 2001.

Were other people not committing suicide? Yes, they were but the rate was 47 per cent higher among farmers in 2011.

Even in farmer suicides there is a 'Big Five' set of states—as if it were the GDP—and these are Madhya Pradesh, Andhra Pradesh, Maharashtra, Chhattisgarh and Karnataka. They count for two-thirds of all farmer suicides in India.

India's most prominent food activist, Devinder Sharma, says his problem is no longer Walmart or India's desire to bring in big international retail like Walmart, which he believes will be disastrous for

Farmers have been committing suicide at the rate of one every half hour since 2001

the country's farmers. He lists the two foremost myths about Walmart:

1. It creates jobs. Walmart in the US has a turnover of $400 billion, roughly the same as the total size of Indian retail. Walmart employs 2.1 million people. Indian retail employs around 44 million across 12 million shops.
2. Walmart increases farm income. And yet, the US continues to give massive subsidies to its farmers. In 2012, the insurance subsidy against loss of crop or income alone was $14 billion (around Rs 877 crore)—7 times what was given in 2000.

But in the run-up to these polls, Sharma is looking for a real rethink, a real alternative economic thinking. 'So if the Congress says that migration from the village is the only future and the BJP says the same thing, how are they different? Where is the person who is saying maybe we can improve the villages to best sustainable standards in the world? Is it a competition of my SEZ (Special Economic Zone) versus your SEZ?' asks Sharma.

Sharma says he is looking for a real debate on what our economic choices really are, to questions like: where do we really want to buy our food? Do we believe that more and more farmland should be taken away to build highways and industrial corridors? What does that do to our food security? How are we going to ensure that all Indians in the future have food to eat? Do we have a plan for our future food security? Do we believe that importing food is our grand plan to ensure that everyone has food to eat in the future?

Mankombu Sambasivan (M.S.) Swaminathan, one of the pioneers of India's Green Revolution, once told me that the world of the future will be dominated by those with food more than those with guns. Which side does India want to see itself?

31. Food, Rotting

One of the most interesting global reports I read in 2013 was the *Global Food—Waste Not Want Not* report of the Institution of Mechanical Engineers.

It says India wastes 21 million tonnes of wheat each year due to lack of proper storage. This is equal to the total annual production of Australia.

India wastes 21 million tonnes of wheat each year due to lack of proper storage

It also says 40 per cent of all fruits and vegetables produced in the country are also wasted.

32. People, Hungry

India improved its position on the Global Hunger Index 2013 from being 67th in 2011 to 63rd, two years later, among 120 countries. But it still has the highest number of underweight children under the age of five (around 40 per cent).

The proportion of undernourished Indians has reduced from 21 per cent to 17.5 per cent and the proportion of underweight children has declined from 43.5 per cent to 40 per cent, while under-five mortality dropped from 7.5 per cent to 6 per cent.

This means that the hunger index for India fell from 24 to 21 between 2003 and 2012.

We are acting but are we acting fast enough? Oh, by the way, we are still behind Bangladesh and Pakistan in this.

33. Shelter Free

There are 9.42 lakh homeless people in urban India. That's 1.64 lakh more than in 2001.

This means today, unlike in 2001, the number of urban homeless people exceeds rural homeless. 65 million people in India today live in slums, which is more than the 52 million in 2001.

Maharashtra, the state with the maximum number of people living in slums, has 11 million, Andhra Pradesh follows with 10 million in slums and West Bengal and Uttar Pradesh have more than six million each.

To accommodate all the people who will migrate to cities by 2030, India needs to build 900 million new urban residential areas.

A third of all slum dwellers live in unauthorised slums.

Can they ever be anything but a vote bank?

34. Birth/Death

India's maternal death rate has shown signs of improvement from 280 per 100,000 births to the current 230. In the same period, China went from 44 to 38.

Something similar is happening in infant mortality too. In this, numbers in India fell from 57 per 100,000 to 50 while China is at 17.

Some of our neighbours, like Bangladesh and Sri Lanka, are beating us at this even as we talk about our regional super power status.

Rates of DPT (diphtheria, pertussis and tetanus) immunization in India is 72 per cent compared to 82 per cent in Nepal, 96 per cent in Botswana, 96 per cent in Bangladesh and 99 per cent in Sri Lanka.

According to 2011 calculations by the Organisation for Economic Cooperation and Development (OECD), India spent around 3.9 per cent on heath care—lower than any OECD country and much less than the OECD average of 9.3 per cent.

World Bank statistics show that we have 0.9 beds per 1,000 of population (and that's why it is not surprising that in our hospitals so many patients actually sleep on the floor) compared to the global average of 2.9 per 1,000.

World Bank statistics show that we have 0.9 hospital beds per 1,000 of population compared to the global average of 2.9 per 1,000

OECD statistics also show that in 2011, India had only 0.7 physicians per 1,000 population, well below the OECD average of 3.2. There was less than one nurse per 1,000 population in India in 2010, much lower than the average of 8.7 in OECD countries. And the number of hospital beds in India was 0.6 per 1,000 population in 2010, much lower also than the OECD average of 4.8 beds per 1,000 population.

The World Bank calculates that India is one of the countries in the world where people have to spend maximum from their pocket in private healthcare—as opposed to government paid healthcare or insurance—and from 2008 to 2011 we moved from 87.1 per cent privately paid for to 86 per cent. China is at 78.8 per cent.

The data journalism initiative, India Spend, calculated in 2012 that rural India has a shortage of over 12,300 specialist doctors and a shortfall of 9,814 health centres.

The World Health Organisation (WHO) estimates that at least 3.2 per cent of Indians are falling below the poverty line each year because they cannot afford healthcare.

And what is India losing in the process? In 2000, India lost 9.2 million productive years due to heart disease alone and is likely to lose 17.9 million years in 2030—just to get a sense, that's 570 per cent and 900 per cent more than the US.

The Harvard School of Public Health estimates that economic losses to India due to non-communicable diseases will be around $6.2 trillion between 2012 and 2030.

According to WHO estimates, India has 21 per cent of the 'disease burden' of the world, even though it only has 17 per cent of the global population. A World Bank report calculated in 2010 that India was losing up to 6 per cent of its GDP in premature deaths and preventable illness.

As early as 2007, a PricewaterhouseCoopers and Assocham (The Associated Chambers of Commerce and Industry in India) report had warned that 53 per cent of all deaths in India come from chronic disease, as do 44 per cent of disability-adjusted life years. By 2020, such deaths will rise to more than eight million, from four million before 2000.

Even if you take some slightly higher estimates, India's total expenditure on health is 4.2 per cent of GDP, the current public expenditure is only at about 1.2 per cent of GDP. With abysmal public health infrastructure and a largely exploitative insurance system, 70 per cent of healthcare spend is 'out of pocket expenditure' and mostly 'at the point of service'. This basically means, unlike in civilised parts of the world where you get treated for illness first and then either the government pays for the treatment or you can leave it to the insurance company to be settled later, in India most people have to pay immediately and out of their own pocket. And in most cases, unless they pay immediately, they get zero treatment. India remains among the five countries with the lowest public health spending in the world. One more thing happens because of this—it makes the poor even poorer.

How many votes does health deserve?

35. The Fat of the Land

Harvard research shows that in 2005, nearly 14 per cent of Indian women, between the ages of 18 and 49, were overweight or obese, with higher rates among urban women (25 per cent) than rural women (8 per cent). The rate of overweight and obesity in women, overall, increased by 3.5 per cent a year from 1998 to 2005.

In 2007, some studies showed that about 5 per cent of all Indians were obese. By 2012, some reports suggest that 36 per cent of Indians are overweight, as are 70 per cent of urban youth.

The world's leading medical journal, *Lancet*, is more conservative and has said in a report that 7.3 per cent of India's population is overweight and 1.2 per cent is obese.

Between 1998 and 2005, obesity rates in India increased 20 per cent and have risen significantly since then. The economic correlation seems to be that a 10 per cent increase in GDP causes a 6 per cent reduction in the stunted growth in children but also 7 per cent rise in overweight people.

By 2030, around 12.9 per cent of Indians are likely to be obese

By 2030, around 12.9 per cent of Indians are likely to be obese.

Greater economic prosperity, cheaper cars, more processed food—and no exercise—is creating a unique situation of extreme hunger and extreme obesity simultaneously in the country.

In Britain, Canada and America, among other countries, there is a vigorous debate on the impact of junk food on children, especially in schools, and whether state policies should restrict it. Do our politicians have an opinion on this?

36. When In Pain, Fake It

India, along with China, leads the world in fake, sub-standard, spurious drugs. Government estimates suggest that less than 1 per cent of medicines sold in India are fake and less than 10 per cent are substandard, but other independent estimates of fakes go up to 10 per cent or 12 per cent.

The medical journal *Lancet* says, 7 per cent of all anti-malarial drugs sold in India are spurious. This is particularly worrying because 70 per cent Indians are at risk from malaria.

In a now well-known study done by Roger Bate, a fellow of the American Enterprise Institute, in 2009, across five categories of medicines and across 52 different pharmacies in Delhi and Chennai, it was found that in Delhi 12 per cent of the pills were substandard, in Chennai it was 5 per cent and 2 per cent of the pills had no active ingredient.

7 per cent of all anti-malarial drugs sold in India are spurious. 70 per cent Indians are at risk from malaria

In 2013, a CNN-IBN report unearthed one case of a company in Himachal Pradesh—Vardhaman Pharmaceuticals. The license of the company lapsed in 2009 but it continued to run a full-fledged factory, which operated only in the night, and supply fake drugs to the central government and to Tripura, Uttar Pradesh and Chhattisgarh.

When, following an alert from the Tripura government, the factory was raided, 700 cartons of medicines, including injections for children were found. In another factory of the company in Haryana, raw materials for medicines were found lying beside animal fodder.

The national initiative against piracy and counterfeiting of the Federation of Indian Chambers of Commerce and Industry has said that of the medicines sold in India, around 15 per cent to 20 per cent are fake. Who is going to stop this?

37. When In Need, Sell a Kidney

In spite of the Human Organ Transplantation Act of 1994, India's underground organ transplant market is 'resurging', says the World Health Organisation, as organs are taken regularly from local donors, often economically poor donors who are paid a pittance (sometimes barely $5,000 in a $130,000–$150,000 deal).

2,000 Indians sell a kidney every year

Around 2,000 Indians sell a kidney every year, estimates the Voluntary Health Association of India.

How can we have an election based on development if we still have a country where the poor have to sell their organs?

38. One for One Lakh

A recent study done by the Harvard School of Public Health found that India has only one operation theatre per 100,000 people.

While south east Asia had 2.6 operation theatres per one lakh people, India shared the dubious distinction with Pakistan of having 1.3 operation theatres (once again that fraction, imagine someone who has access to the 0.3 of an operation theatre) for every lakh of people.

How does this compare with rest of the world? Eastern Europe has 25.1 per 100,000, Western Europe 14.7 and North America and Australasia 14.3.

Half the operating rooms in India do not have functioning oxygen monitors.

Also, nearly half of all operating theatres in South Asia—largely India and Pakistan—do not have bare minimum equipment like a pulse oximeter, which indirectly measures oxygen saturation in the blood.

What's the shortfall of this equipment in Europe? 9 per cent; 7 per cent in Latin America and just 0.2 per cent in Asia Pacific.

Now how many operating theatres could we build on the

amount of black money that will be spent in this election? Hundreds? Thousands? Lakh? When will we get a politician who will put operating theatres not only in his campaign promises but also in his post-win delivery?

39. Why Have We Stopped Talking about HIV/AIDS?

India has more than 2 million people living with HIV, says the National Aids Control Organisation. 86 per cent of all Indians who are HIV-positive are between the ages of 15 and 49. Children under 15 years of age make up 7 per cent of the infections.

There has been a 57 per cent fall in the yearly rate of new HIV infections among adults in India. In 2000, there were 274,000 new cases which fell to 116,000 in 2011.

But as UNICEF points out, India's worries are far from over. In terms of numbers of individual patients, India is still home to the third largest number of people living with HIV in the world. Women account for 40 per cent of infections.

India is still home to the third largest number of people living with HIV in the world. Women account for 40 per cent of infections

Anjali Gopalan is the head of one of the world's most influential sexuality and AIDS organisations, the Naz Foundation. It's the same organisation whose law suit led to the demolition of Section 377 of the Indian Penal Code, a residue from the colonial era which made same sex sexual intercourse a crime and 'against the order of nature'. In 2009, the Delhi High Court ruled that Section 377 offended the fundamental right to equality and therefore treating consensual homosexual sex between adults as a crime was a violation of fundamental rights protected by the Constitution.

Gopalan worries about what she is seeing on the ground. 'The age of infected patients is growing younger, often 13 and 14-year-olds. We still have babies being born with HIV and the public communication against AIDS seems to have nearly stopped. I barely see anything anymore. And I fear that this is just the sort of complacency that leads to an epidemic.'

The worry here is not just about AIDS and the number of patients but about the way Indian society looks at AIDS, looks at homosexuality, and that remains a dark and jaundiced point of view.

Ideally what Gopalan wants is Indian candidates going into an election must come out with what their stand is on homosexuality. In America, for instance, and many other parts of the Western world, stance on homosexuality is part of the election manifestos. 'There are many younger politicians who have homosexual friends and acquaintances and who have progressive points of view in private but not one of them have the courage to take a public stand.'

So Gopalan waits for a tipping point—like Milind Deora's tweet on convicted politicians in Parliament and, later, Rahul Gandhi's outburst—even as she cringes at campy, ridiculous depictions of homosexuality in popular culture.

'When is that sort of inflection point going to come for the human rights of the gay community? I believe this is the election to question such prejudices if we are really talking about change. A lot of ugly viewpoints come out as soon as you talk about marriage rights for homosexuals and the right to adopt children or inherit property and it is very worrying. Yet, these are the things that must be asked of candidates—where do they stand on these vital issues of human rights? Will that inflection point come during these polls? I hope so.'

Days after I spoke to her, her worst fears seemed to have come true when India's Supreme Court overturned the Delhi High Court judgment and upheld Section 377. As this book went to print, there were protests from every part of India against this regressive judgment.

40. A Drugged Punjab

Punjab's yellow fields hide a deeper menace.

A study by the state department of Social Security Development of Women and Children has found that around 67 per cent of rural households in Punjab had at least one drug addict in the family.

There is also at least one death due to drug overdose each week in the region. Most addicts are between 16 and 35 years. An entire generation in Punjab, the food heartland of India, is being lost to drugs.

Some reports suggest that around 70 per cent of all youth in Punjab have a drug problem and in the state elections held in 2012, the Election Commission noted that some candidates even gave away drugs free to win votes. During the polls, around 110 pounds of heroin was seized.

Sixty per cent of all illegal drugs seized in India are captured in Punjab, which is the biggest gateway for drugs from Afghanistan and Pakistan to come into India.

The Daulewala region of Moga in Punjab is often called the drug capital of Punjab. Reports suggest that in an area of

400 households, 390 cases of Narcotic Drugs and Psychotropic Substances (NDPS) Act are registered on residents.

The one top national leader who has spoken directly about the drug issue in Punjab is Rahul Gandhi, who mentioned it in speeches in 2012 and 2013 which caused, as expected, a series of denials from local leaders in Punjab.

41. The High in Kerala

Alcohol is to Kerala what drugs is to Punjab.

Wholesale alcohol supply monopoly earns the Kerala government 20 per cent of its tax revenues. There are 384 state-run liquor shops which serve more than 200 customers every hour, 11 hours a days, seven days a week, and this is apart from the supply to 700 private bars and 5,000 toddy shops.

Reports suggest that folks in Kerala drink 8.3 litres of alcohol a year, more than even Punjab (7.9 litres) and much higher than the national average of 5.7 litres. But there's a flip side—alcohol abuse causes 44 per cent of Kerala's road accidents, 19 per cent of hospital stays and 80 per cent of divorces. Alcohol abuse is a major cause of mental illness—in 2011, the state had the second highest number of suicides.

The ruling Congress government increased the drinking age from 18 to 21 and got bars to agree to open only at 8 am, but many of them complained that that was too late; how would they get the customers wanting the dawn toddy unless they opened at dawn!

Are the Kerala MPs talking about this in their election campaign?

42. No 1 in the World

Around 40 per cent of Indians would die of heart diseases by 2020 compared to 24 per cent in 1990, and doctors in our country now say that with three million people dying of heart diseases each year, we will soon be the heart disease capital of the world.

We also have around 40 million diabetes patients and are also about to become—if not already become—the diabetes capital of the world.

With 15 to 20 million asthma patients and more than 20 per cent of the world's tuberculosis patients, we could also be called the lung disease capital of the world. For instance, in India, one person dies of cancer every 50 seconds. India has more cases of oral cancer than pretty much anywhere in world and breast cancer is now the country's fastest growing disease. The Harvard School of Public Health calculates that India will lose $20 billion (Rs 1,254,20 crore) between 2012 and 2030 to breast cancer. India has the highest number of tuberculosis patients in the world. But even then, 930,000 of them are missed

In India, one person dies of cancer every 50 seconds

by the health system and don't get treated. Do you know how many people died of tuberculosis in India in 2012? 270,000.

Read the manifestos these polls carefully.

43. Business, *Shijhness*

How easy is it to do business in India? After all, if a country is going to become the next economic powerhouse of the world, it must do business, mustn't it?

There is actually a World Bank index that studies this every year across more than 180 countries. It is called the Ease of Doing Business Ranking.

In 2013, India's ease of doing business rank was 131. In 2014, it fell to 134. Now this ease of doing business is divided into many criteria and each of these have a ranking. Here's how India fared in 2012 and 2013:

Topic	*2014*	*2013*
Starting a Business	179	177
Dealing with construction permits	182	183
Getting electricity	111	110
Registering property	92	91
Getting credit	28	24

Topic	*2014*	*2013*
Protecting investors	34	32
Paying taxes	158	159
Trading across borders	132	129
Enforcing contracts	186	186
Resolving insolvency	121	119

Here's how India's rank has changed from 2006 to 2013—116, 124, 120, 132, 133, 134, 132, 132. We have actually slid considerably.

Which countries are ranked much higher than India? Some of the most restive in the world—Pakistan (107), Egypt (109) and Ethiopia (127) among many others.

There's another interesting statistic that this survey throws up. It's called DTF or Distance To Frontier. The frontier is the average of best performing countries or the environments easiest to do business and where 100 is the frontier and 0 is the worst performance.

And in this is the bit of good news, India's 'distance from the frontier' of perfection has decreased. From 2006 to 2013, we have moved from 41.4 to 51.9.

In the 2013 annual Global Competitiveness Report, by the World Economic Forum (WEF), India was positioned 31 places below China

There is another ranking worth looking at, something where we scored our lowest ever in 2013. It is called the Global Competitiveness Report, done every year by the World Economic Forum (WEF). India scored 60th in this in 2013—31 places below China.

Why?

The reasons don't surprise me, and they won't surprise you. We live with them every day. Our transport, information and communications technology and energy infrastructure are abysmal. Or as the WEF said in its report 'remains largely insufficient and ill-adapted to the needs of the economy'. Oh and yes, here's something worth noting: in 2006, the competitiveness gap between India and China was 6 places. Now it's 31. In the same time, Indonesia has jumped 12 places to 38th, far ahead of India.

(It should be mentioned that India protested against its ease of doing business ranking of 2013, saying that some of the issues were peculiar to the place where the company the survey chose to study was based in. Which city was that? India's financial capital—Mumbai.)

Also we ranked 119 among 177 countries on the Heritage Foundation and the Wall Street Journal's economic freedom index in 2013.

44. Bambai

18 million people. 6,000 people die on its local train tracks every year. At least 500 just fall off, maybe more. If you live in Bombay, or call it Mumbai, you know that the city is dying. It has finally come to that place from where cities rarely ever return, they collapse even further to riots, or abandoned.

India's financial capital is so disgustingly, disturbingly, despairingly crumbling that every adjective seems pitiable before its Dantesque mess.

Local trains carry 6.1 million passengers every day. The Bandra-Worli Sea Link was to take two and a half years. It actually took 10. Its river Mithi—a 15 kilometre snaking drain that sums up everything wrong with the city—remains one of the ugliest and most foul water bodies in any city, anywhere in the world.

During the 2005 unprecedented rains, the river flooded and drowned the city shutting it down for days. Mumbai recovered but remains scarred as it does from two of the biggest terror attacks ever on Indian soil—the series of bomb blasts on local trains that killed more than 200 people and the attacks in six places in 2008 that killed 164.

Compare the banks of the Mithi river with the world class urban regeneration that Ahmedabad has been able to do to with its own Sabarmati riverfront and it is easy to see how things can—and also refuse to—work in India.

The 2011 census shows that 33 per cent of homes in Mumbai and 45 per cent in the suburbs of the city have no toilets. So infamous is Mumbai's inability to get itself weather-functioning roads that one well-known politician from the city has claimed that the potholes,which constantly make headlines in the city, are spoiling its 'image'. This image was of a city that will eventually become as spick and span as Shanghai and politicians—before the 2005 floods and the terror attacks—would talk of Mumbai becoming Shanghai. There has even been a Bollywood film on the dystopian nightmare that is Mumbai's politics, with the governance and infrastructure mockingly called Shanghai. 60 per cent or more of all people living in Mumbai live in slums.

60 per cent or more of all people living in Mumbai live in slums

After the 2008 terror attacks, a filmmaker called Ram Gopal Verma went to 'see the spots' with the then chief minister. Verma later made a film called 26/11, 'encashing', as Bollywood would say, on the attacks. It flopped.

The number of vehicles has grown by 50 per cent between 2005 and 2012 in Mumbai but the roads have barely grown 10 per cent.

Bombay First, the citizens group that campaigns for a better Mumbai, often says it is a 21st century city running on 19th century infrastructure.

Seventeen agencies are supposedly responsible for maintaining Mumbai.

Any hope? Well, the metro rail system has just started, as has a mono rail.

45. Dilli

Earlier in this book, we looked at how safe India's capital and adjoining areas are for women. It is so critical an issue that it merits separate mention. But that's not the only thing gone critically wrong about Delhi.

Almost no property can be bought or sold in the capital of India without paying large sums—sometimes up to 70 per cent and almost never below 30 per cent—completely illegally in cash.

Delhi, which also has around 18 million people, has 49 per cent of its people or half its population living in slums. Only 25 per cent of the population live in planned areas and have access to regular sewage disposal. It has no real breakthrough idea to treat its sewage.

Interestingly enough, rag pickers continue to be one of Delhi's primary ways to disposing waste. Delhi still has 80,000 to 100,000 rag pickers who collect around 50 kg per person per day,which takes care of between 1,200 to 1,500 tonnes of garbage a day.

The city has 7.4 million cars and 1,200 more are added every day. The Centre for Science and Environment says it would take the same space as 310 football fields being added each year to keep pace with Delhi's parking demands. Delhi today has almost as much parking space (10 per cent of the land area) as green area (11 per cent).

Last heard, of the 41 planned parking projects, only one had opened.

According to the Bureau of Police Research and Development, Delhi comes second after Punjab in using its understaffed police force to guard VIPs. There are 5,183 cops being used just for VIP protection in Delhi even though the city's police force to population ratio is one cop to 253 people.

Delhi also has a pitiable power situation. Electricity prices have been increased by the Delhi Electricity Regulatory Commission (DERC) four times in the last two years, and yet, power cuts abound.

Last heard, Anil Ambani's Reliance Infrastructure owed more than Rs 3,300 crore to the power generation and transmission companies owned by the Delhi government and received a letter from the chief minister's office demanding immediate fixing.

Greenpeace, the not-for-profit environment watchdog, says Delhi has achieved barely one per cent of its renewable energy targets.

Tiny piece of good news: a 345-W solar energy project was set up in 2013. And some pressure on the cops have reduced since the Aam Aadmi Party ministers don't take any security.

There are 5,183 cops being used just for VIP protection in Delhi, even though the city's police force to population ratio is 1 cop to 253 people

46. The Many Us

By 2025, India will have more people than China. By 2050, it will have 1.7 billion people.

The good news is that fertility rate—or the number of babies a woman can have during her life—is falling as is the population growth rate, especially in southern India. But the north is still a problem area.

If you think that this is a 'demographic dividend' just look at the numbers of Indians without toilets and the air pollution and the stress of drinking water numbers earlier in this book.

Which politician or political party ever says that population is a critical area for us? Why do they only want to believe that somehow all our adding millions will add to the fortunes of the country? The truth is, it won't, they won't. And here we are looking at a coming era of never-before pressure on our resources—natural, environmental, sociological and financial.

47. Young Country? Well, Not That Much

You might not hear enough about this but India's population is not exploding in the way it used to. And many parts of the country actually have ageing populations that match Europe and Scandinavia.

In 2001, about 54 per cent of Indians were younger than 25 years; in 2011, this fell to 50 per cent. That's why we are still talking about half of all Indians being under the age of 50.

Our population is finally stabilizing. Well, for one, we aren't producing as many babies. The total fertility rate (TFR) which calculates the number of children a woman is able to have in a lifetime has dropped in the last 35 years from 4.5 to 2.4. Adjusted to India's child and infant mortality rates, this is approximately around the international standards of net reproduction rate of 2.1—which means that a woman would bear at an average of two children in a lifetime. According to the Population Projection Report of 2006, this would fall to 2 between 2021 and 2025. Nine Indian states—Maharashtra, Karnataka, Delhi, West Bengal, Punjab, Himachal Pradesh, Andhra Pradesh, Tamil Nadu and Kerala—have TFR rates of 2 or less. Tamil Nadu and

Kerala are at the lowest at 1.7. Internationally, 1.7 is the TFR of Canada, while 1.9 is the TFR of Norway and Sweden.

In 2001, 7.4 per cent of the Indian population were above 60 years of age. The Ministry of Statistics and Programme Implementation estimates that this will rise to 12.4 per cent by 2026.

By 2050, there will most likely be only 3 working Indians for every dependent elderly compared to 8 working citizens at the moment

Now the other thing to understand in this is the old age dependency ratio which is basically a ratio between the working younger population and the dependent elderly population. As this ratio grows, the working force is under greater pressure to provide assistance and support to the growing numbers of dependent elderly. Between 1961 and 2001, this ratio grew in India from 10.9 per cent to 13.1 per cent. This is expected to rise to 32.8 per cent by 2050.

By 2050, there will most likely be only 3 working Indians for every dependent elderly compared to 8 working citizens at the moment.

Also, 65 per cent of the elderly had to depend on others (children, spouse, relatives) for day to day maintenance. What we need to remember here is that the elderly in India are far poorer at an average than the elderly in the West. There is a gender problem here too; less than 20 per cent of elderly women are financially independent.

48. Who Let the Jobs Out?

If you still like to think that India has a demographic dividend, you should know some statistics from the National Association of Software and Services Companies (Nasscom).

It says that 75 per cent of technical graduates (like engineering or computer science students) and 80 per cent of general graduates are so poorly trained that they cannot be hired in any software company or, largely, even call centres.

Then look at what Pratham, one of India's biggest education NGOs, found. They surveyed 13,000 schools in rural India and discovered that 50 per cent of the students in class five cannot read the text at the level of class two. It also found that 40 per cent of ten-year-olds cannot do basic subtraction.

In a recent report called Employability and Skill Set of Newly Graduated Engineers in India, the World Bank said that 64 per cent of employers were not satisfied with the skill sets of fresh engineering graduates.

That's why IDFC's India Infrastructure Report of 2012 says 45 per cent of all graduates earn less than Rs 75,000 a year.

Of the nearly 13 million people joining the workforce every

year in India, less than 10 per cent have any skills and many can barely read.

Of the nearly 13 million people joining the workforce every year in India, less than 10 percent have any skills and many can barely read

Kiran Mazumdar-Shaw of Biocon voices her concern over the fact that a key issue remains unaddressed in this election campaign—sustainable skill development and job creation. She says, 'How are we ensuring government investment to ensure that it brings skills and capabilities for the people that in turn generate livelihood?

'The crisis that India faces is not so much a lack of jobs but a lack of people who have the right skills for the jobs that are available. That's my primary objection with the MNREGA and the Food Security Bill too—if you leave aside the leakage allegations for a moment—does it help people to apply their learning productively? Is there any training that is intrinsic to—MNREGA? Why can't government and industry formulate a plan to use MNREGA workers productively where skills are taught by industry and the—MNREGA 100 days wages is used as an employment subsidy by industry who will pay for the balance 200 days? Why are we failing to bring about such crucial linkages? We need to provide productive, meaningful employment for millions of people, and millions more are being added to the workforce every year. We cannot address this by paying wages for unproductive jobs. Handing out money has its use in poverty alleviation but beyond that there has to be a plan on how to ensure that people are integrated into the labour force.

'The key thing to understand is that we have to evaluate government policy on the parameters of collective capacity building. And most government policies do not seem to be in this direction. That is the debate we ought to be having. Otherwise we will face an even greater economic challenge in the future. And capacity building also means infrastructure. Bengaluru, where I live, is a prime example of this. There has been a complete lack of thought in the development of Bengaluru, as with many other cities, and infrastructure has not developed in tandem with the population growth. Therefore our capacity for urban renewal is very poor and urban migration from rural towns and the future of our cities should be a critical debate in these polls. We are not hearing enough about governance but only about politics and that has to change. Job creation must be a focus for the next government.'

'The crisis that India faces is not so much a lack of jobs but a lack of people who have the right skills for the jobs that are available. That's my primary objection with the MNREGA and the Food Security Bill too—if you leave aside the leakage allegations for a moment—does it help people learn that they can use productively? Why is it that government and industry cannot formulate a plan to use MNREGA workers where skills are taught and they are paid more than what the Rs 100 that the scheme entails? Why are we failing to bring about such crucial linkages? We need to provide productive, satisfying employment for millions of people, and millions more are being added to the workforce every year. We cannot do this just by handing out money,' says Mazumdar-Shaw. 'Handing out money has its use but beyond that there has to be a plan on how do you ensure that people are integrated to the labour force?'

So how is the government faring in its training programme? The National Skill Development Corporation (NSDC) and other ministries could only fulfill 16.5 per cent of their target for 2012–13. The need was to train 8.5 million people. Only 1.4 million could be trained.

A report by the Federation of Indian Chamber of Commerce and Industry (FICCI) and Ernst & Young in 2011 counted 40 million registered on Indian employment exchanges, but said 0.2 per cent get jobs every year; 80 per cent of all Indians do not have the skills to get a ready job.

80 per cent of all Indians do not have the skills to get a ready job

The target is to train 350 million people by 2022.

'What is expected to happen by 2022 if this target is not met? A series of shortfalls in employees in various industries—103 million in infrastructure, 35 million in auto, more than 26 million in textiles, more than 17 million in organised retail and more than 12 million in healthcare. It is a list that talks about India shutting down, especially since it shows a 5.8 million shortfall even in education and skill development. Who will train the teachers?

The key thing to understand is that we have to evaluate government policy on the parameters of collective capacity building. And most government policy does not seem to be in that direction. That is the debate we ought to be having. Otherwise we will face even greater economic worry in the future. And capacity building also means infrastructure. Bengaluru, where I live, is a prime example of this. There has been a complete lack of thought in the development of Bengaluru, as with many other cities, and no service has developed in tandem with the population. Therefore our capacity for urban renewal is very poor and migration and the future of our cities should be a critical debate in these polls. We are not hearing enough about governance but only about politics and that has to change.'

49. Mystery of the Missing Teachers

We don't have enough teachers. Some estimates suggest that the shortfall of trained teachers in India could be as high as 1.4 million.

There are missing departments of education in 12 of 40 central universities in the country. Uttar Pradesh needs nearly 300,000 teachers, Bihar needs 260,000 and Bengal around 100,000.

In a curious turn of events, India now has a Right to Education but not enough teachers to deliver that right,especially since even among the teachers who are being hired 20 per cent do not fulfill standards of the National Council for Teachers' Education.

And what about the teachers who are there?

A 2004 research done by a group of scholars from the World Bank and Harvard University across 20 states and 3,700 schools shows that 25 per cent of Indian teachers were absent from schools and only half were really teaching.

In Punjab, there were even instance of teachers who had been absent for seven years!

In Uttar Pradesh, the situation was getting worse. According to the Annual Status of Education Report (ASER) by the NGO

Pratham, 19 per cent of primary school teachers were not present in 2011. This had increased from 8 per cent in 2007. At the upper primary level, the missing teacher rate had doubled from around 10 per cent to 20 per cent.

This naturally meant that only 53.1 per cent of primary and 46.9 per cent of upper primary level schools had teachers in full strength but here too the numbers had fallen sharply from 70 per cent in 2007. This in a country where 4 per cent of children never go to school, 58 per cent don't complete primary school and 90 per cent don't complete school. Only 10 per cent go to college.

50. The Unbanked

World Bank data from 2011 shows only 35 per cent of Indians above the age of 15 years have an account at a formal financial institution. Only 26 per cent of the women above 15 years have this facility.

Only 27 per cent of the bottom 40 per cent of poorest Indians have an account at a formal financial institution (what the data does not say explicitly is the rest of the story, which is that most people, who don't have such access, depend on the 'informal sector' or usually the vicious trap of moneylenders).

Around 40% of households have no access to any form of banking at all. The ratio of total bank credit outstanding to GDP is only about 57% as against over 140% in East Asia and the Pacific. Insurance premia account for less than 1% of GDP, which is only about one-third of the international average.

Only 8 per cent of Indians get their wages directly into a bank account, and 4 per cent get their due government funds in an account (though this may have gone up slightly after the start of direct cash transfers). Just about 12 per cent save money in a bank account.

A major government thrust towards financial inclusion started in 2010 but before that something worrying happened—between 1991 and 2007 the number of banked centres actually fell from 35,236 to 34,471. The number of rural branches also fell from 35,206 to 30,409.

But there is also some good news. Between 2010 and 2013, around 268,000 banking centres were opened in villages.

Full rural bank branches (as opposed to limited service centres) rose by 7,400.

About 109 million savings deposit accounts were added.

Around 9.48 million farming households and 2.24 million non-farming households in rural areas got small entrepreneurial credit during this period.

51. Mind the Gap

Ever wondered what the modern social reasoning behind India's gender violence and divide is?

The World Economic Forum has the answer. It ranked India at 101 among 136 countries on how efficiently and equitably resources and opportunities are divided between men and women across the areas of the economy, education, politics and health.

The good news is that India ranks a very high 9th spot for political power division and equity between men and women, but a dismal 135th for health and survival. We fared pretty poorly in economic participation (124th) and 120th in education.

India has the lowest rank among BRICS nations, even though we have skimmed up from the 105th position in 2012. China is at 69th, Russia at 61st and Brazil at 62nd.

52. Nationally Risk Averse

In the WEF 2013 Global Risks Report, India ranked last, among the world's major economies, in how much it was prepared for environmental risks and second last for economic risks. Just so that we know what these risks are, two of the most worrying risks in the next decade, said the WEF, were severe income disparity and major systemic financial failure.

Both sound like they are perfectly apt for India. Not only do we have severe income divide but also our major banks are under tremendous debt pressure.

The economies surveyed in this report were: America, China, the UK, Switzerland, Russia, Germany, Italy, India, Brazil and Japan.

We fared slightly better—at 6th position—in the government's risk management effectiveness but second lowest once again in global competitiveness.

The most worrying risks for the world according to the WEF are: severe income disparity, chronic fiscal imbalances, rising greenhouse emissions, water supply crises and failing to manage an ageing population.

53. The Bribes of the Poor

We know all about the bribes of the rich—scam this, scandal that, sometimes, a little file shifting in between—but what about the bribes paid by the poor?

The Delhi think-tank Centre for Media Studies, along with Transparency International found the answer. It showed that around 50 million BPL or below poverty line households paid as much as Rs 8,830 million (883 crore) in bribes in a year to get state services with the police taking the maximum amount—half the households surveyed had to pay the police at the very first step, which is registering their complaint.

What kind of services are people paying for? Eleven key types: the police, banking, housing, forests, the national rural employment guarantee scheme and land records and registration, and then some more basic ones like the public distribution system, water supply, electricity, health services and education.

50 million households, below the poverty line, paid as much as Rs 8,830 million (883 crore) in bribes in a year to get state services

Apart from the police, the other utterly rotten service which the poor have to pay for is land records and registration. The study said that rather than a trickle down to the poor, in many cases, economic benefits have trickled up to powerful state beneficiaries.

54. Power/Less

The blackout in 2012 shut off power for nearly 600 million Indians. But even in everyday situations, around three hundred million Indians do not have even an intermittent supply of electricity. This in spite of that fact that India has the fifth largest electrical system in the world with a capacity of around 180 gigawatt (GW). By 2035, India's electricity needs are likely to double.

Most of our power needs are fulfilled by thermal energy sources like coal, gas and oil (around 68 per cent), followed by hydro or water which accounts for a little more than renewable sources like solar and wind, and finally some 2 per cent comes from nuclear sources.

India has the fifth largest coal reserves (though of largely poor quality) in the world but coal imports have trebled in a decade to $1.5 trillion (Rs 94, 065,00 crore) a year. According to the International Energy Agency, by 2017, energy imports would rise faster in India than anywhere else in the world and India's energy imports would overtake that of the United States. and that if we want growth at 9 per cent every year, we need to add 20,000 megawatts (MW) of power each year.

We import three-quarters of our oil. We are stuck with a dispute in our largest natural gas field operated by Reliance Industries which has had a critical problem of production shortfalls. With the coal block allocation scam, the accusatory fingers have travelled from big businessmen like Naveen Jindal and Kumaramangalam Birla to the former coal secretary who has in turn pointed fingers at the prime minister's office.

The good news is that plans are afoot to build the world's largest solar power plant in Rajasthan near the Sambhar Lake to generate 4,000 MW of electricity. In the last three years, India has put up 1.8 GW of solar power plants and another 2.3 GW is expected in the coming months. The target: 20,000 MW of solar power by 2022.

The two top performing states in this are Gujarat, which has completed 800 MW of installations, and Tamil Nadu which has a target of 3,000 MW by 2015.

At the moment, India has 1,759 MW of solar power connected to grids.

Wind energy has a potential to deliver around 80,000 MW but only about 17,000 MW is installed at the moment.

India has about 20 nuclear reactors in six operating nuclear plants but plans to generate up to 63,000 MW by 2032 (at the moment it's 4,780 MW) seems stalled, following local protests against proposed nuclear power sites including in Jaitapur in Maharashtra and Kundankulam in Tamil Nadu after the Fukushima disaster in Japan in 2011.

The time has come to ask the question—who has the vision to implement a plan that will bring electricity to all Indians?

55. The Shit Hits the Train

Some estimates suggest that India still has more than 300,000 manual scavengers. Some others have even more drastic accounts. According to the International Dalit Solidarity Network, 1.3 million Dalits, mostly women, earn their living by working as manual scavengers. In some cases the payment is one rupee a day.

Manual scavenging is the task of cleaning 'dry' toilets and carrying the excreta away to a dump, usually in baskets.

One of the key offenders in this is the Indian Railways which still has trains that have systems that dump excreta of passengers directly onto railway tracks which are then cleaned by hired manual scavengers.

A new, more powerful, law called the Prohibition of Employment as Manual Scavengers and their Rehabilitation Bill has been passed in 2013, making it strictly illegal to employ manual scavengers. It states that all dry toilets will have to be demolished and also provides for rehabilitation of these workers. It was much needed since the last law framed in 1993 saw zero conviction in its history. Before the latest law was passed, Delhi became the first state to ban manual scavenging.

All our democratic pride means nothing as long as there are thousands who have to feed themselves in our country by collecting and cleaning human shit. It means … nothing.

56. Witch Hunt

In 2012, 119 women were killed across Indian states accused of being witches. Since 2008, more than 760 women have been killed after being branded witches.

Two of the worst offending states are Jharkhand and Odisha. In 2012, 26 'witches' were killed in Jharkhand and 32 in Odisha.

Who will stop this?

57. Love in the Time of Murder

There are three key reasons Indians get murdered these days. Two of them are as old as human civilization—personal vendetta or enmity (or, say, why Ram killed Ravan), then there's property dispute (or, say, why the war of Kurukshetra happened) but it is the third that is most worrying.

The National Crime Records Bureau refers to it as love affairs/sexual causes. In 2012, the number of people who were killed due to this was 2,549.

The state with the maximum number of such murders was Andhra Pradesh where 445 people died.

Mostly this is men murdering women, proving once again that India is undergoing a gender war as waves of unprecedented women's emancipation crashes against sullen dams of protracted patriarchy.

Unless violence against women becomes a key focus area of political campaigning and public policy, this will be a long, brutal war where most of the victims will be women.

In 2012, 2,549 people were killed due to love affairs/sexual causes

58. The Labour of a Child

India has nearly 50 lakh child labourers, according to the National Sample Survey Organisation (NSSO). Some of the biggest sectors that employ child labour in India are the diamond industry, silk industry, domestic labour and fireworks manufacture.

The good news is that according to the NSSO there has been a 60 per cent reduction in the number of working children between 2001 and 2011—from 12.6 million to 4.9 million.

Some of the biggest professions which extensively use child labour are the paan, bidi and cigarette industries, construction, spinning and weaving and domestic workers.

Uttar Pradesh alone has 1.7 million child workers.

59. How We Abuse Children

One of the most revelatory studies into child abuse in India was done in 2007 by the Ministry of Women and Child, UNICEF and the NGO, Prayas. It found horrifying things that ought to echo across our politics but more often than not does not.

Here's what it found:

1. Younger children between the ages of 5–12 are the ones most abused.
2. Boys and girls are equally at risk of abuse.
3. The abuser is usually someone trusted and known to the child.
4. 70 per cent of abuse is never reported.
5. Two out of three children are physically abused.
6. Most children physically abused within the family, were abused by parents.
7. Most children don't report physical abuse.
8. Half of all children work all seven days a week.
9. Around 53 per cent children face some form of sexual abuse.

Most children physically abused within the family, were abused by parents

10. The worst offending states in physical and sexual abuse are Assam, Andhra Pradesh, Bihar and Delhi.
11. Nearly half the girls said they wished they were boys.

This is the root of what we believe is going to be our demographic dividend. Generations of abused children will reach adulthood harbouring this kind of trauma deep within them. Is this how we are going to become the next super power?

60. A Dead Woman Every Hour

In 2012, there were 8,233 deaths of women across India, for which the reason was dowry.

Numbers from the National Crime Records Bureau (NCRB) show that women were killed for dowry at the rate of one every hour last year.

Due to greater reporting of cases—or perhaps to an extent a greater greed which has grown along with the Indian growth story—cases of dowry deaths have increased between 2007 and 2012.

In 2007, there were 8,093 dowry deaths, in 2008 it was 8,172, and 8,383 in 2009. In 2010, it was 8,391.

61. Why Do People Kill Themselves in India?

If you look at suicide data from the NCRB, in 2012, a total of 120,488 Indians killed themselves. That's more than a lakh and twenty thousand of us who decided that life was not worth living. Why?

The highest number of people who killed themselves did so because of 'family problems'. Now you might assume these family problems might be financial problems. You would be wrong; bankruptcy and finance-related suicides are separately listed. In fact all the other things one can think of—divorce, dowry, illicit affairs, fall in 'social reputation'. (Poverty, unemployment, physical abuse are also all listed separately.)

Apart from all this, there were more than 30,000 people (30,792 to be precise) dead from 'family problems'. That's the society you and I live in. That's the Indian family values we are so proud of. What are these 'family problems'? Your guess is as good as mine but both you and I have a sneaky, uncomfortable feeling at the moment, don't we, that we might just know what some of these problems are?

The fact is that India today has one of the scariest, most dysfunctional societies in the world where the modern and the traditional, the liberated and the patriarchal, the unfettered and the claustrophobic are colliding with terrible consequences.

And those are not the only numbers in the crime report that are worrying.

'Love affairs' made 3,849 kill themselves in 2012. Failure in examination killed 2,246. Can you imagine? Failing in love and failing in a test caused many Indians so much grief that 6,095 of them just did not want to live!

Reports suggest that between 2006 and 2010, student suicides in India went up from 5,857 to 7,379 or, as the *Times of India* calculated, in 2010, every day, 20 students killed themselves.

What is it about our notions of education, about success that drives people so insane that failure means, literally, the end of their life?

Think about this—if our collapsing societies, destroyed homes and families, suicidal students are not vital conversations on which our politics and governance is based, then what is the value of the politics and why should we debate that governance?

'Suspected or illicit relation' caused another 1,018 people to commit suicide, interestingly almost equally divided between men and women. 'Cancellation/non-settlement of marriage' caused 810 suicides, again almost equally divided between men and women.

Then, 'fall in social reputation' cause 981 suicides. The disturbing thing here—and reason I believe Indian notions of patriarchy must now be reconsidered—nearly 70 per cent of this number were men.

In 2010, 20 students killed themselves every day

62. Road Kill

More people die from road accidents in India than anywhere else in the world. Our country accounts for 10 per cent of all road accident fatalities in the world.

The World Health Organisation (WHO) says death rate per 100,000 population rose in India from 16.8 to 18.9 between 2009 and 2013.

If you look at numbers in 2011, we had 440,123 road accidents and 136,834 people were killed in them. Between 2001 and 2011, death rates from accidents on Indian roads rose by 44.2 per cent.

At the moment, one person dies in a road accident every five minutes in India. By 2020, the number is expected to be one every three minutes.

63. Incredibly, Not Enough Tourists Yet

The Incredible India campaign took India's tourism receipts or money made from tourism from \$3.5 billion (Rs 21,948.5 crore) in 2003 to \$18 billion in 2012.

This meant that India moved up from the 38th spot to the 16th in the Biggest Tourism Spots in the World list. From about 2.7 million tourists in 2003, India now gets around a little more than six-and-a-half million tourists.

But that's actually very little. After all, India gets fewer visitors than Indonesia and Poland, and only two-thirds the number of visitors to Singapore and only a quarter that of Malaysia. Even Ukraine gets around 21 million visitors!

In 2012, when India managed around 6.6 million tourists, Saudi Arabia got 13 million, Morocco 9 million and Poland 13.35 million. China? Well China gets more than 57 million tourists a year.

After the Delhi gang rape in December 2012, tourist footfalls dropped by 25 per cent in 2013 and women tourist numbers fell by 35 per cent.

All this worries Aman Nath, who along with Francis Wacziarg, is the founder of the Neemrana group of restored heritage destinations. 'We keep talking about Indian culture but actually no one cares about it. Our museums are a mess, our crafts and culture is being destroyed every single day and all we really care about is how to make that quick buck.'

What Nath says he finds astonishing in tourism is that ideas that even the government comes up with have absolutely no bearing with what exists on the ground. For instance, this idea of village tourism.

'I look at our villages and I think what on earth are they talking about? We have failed to build toilets in most of them, the roads are often terrible, the drinking water might not be clean—what are these tourist spots that we want to create?' says Nath.

'The perspective of every debate we have is skewed. Our tourism is based not on what we have on the ground (villages that don't even have the basics) but on ideas like, oh, see, see, there is rural tourism in Italy and France! We don't even have toilets! Where are these tourists going to come from to go see villages?'

Our museums are a mess, our crafts and culture is being destroyed every single day and all we really care about is how to make that quick buck

Nath says this election, the fraud in debates needs to stop. 'We have to debate what we have and what we can do better. In most parts of India, this single window clearance is a joke. Just saying incredible India is not enough. We need infrastructure, safety measures from crime and harassment; instead we think just advertising is enough. We need to have an urgent debate about our mindset and what we really need, as opposed to what we think we need.'

64. Low IT Q

In 2013, the International Telecommunication Union ranked India at 121 among 157 nations in how far we have progressed in information and communication technology (ICT).

So much for our great info-tech prowess.

The ranking is based on an ICT Development Index comprising 11 indicators. Among the things taken into account are—internet users per 100 population, wireless and broadband penetration depth, mobile subscriptions and Internet bandwidth used per user.

India has also been ranked at 145 among 200 countries in the Broadband Commission for Digital Development report.

In fact, India is placed among a group of 39 least connected countries. Most other countries in this group of 39 are African nations.

65. The Low Speed Nation

India has the third largest number of Internet users in the world. The Telecom Regulatory Authority of India (TRAI) says we have around 164.81 million users, while the analytics firm, comScore says we have around 74 million. (This is at the time this book was being written and would have increased to a degree in the time taken for it to be published and when you are reading it, but fundamentally the issues remain the same.)

But most of them don't seem to have much of an Internet experience because we are one of the slowest nations in the world. The State of the Report of Akamai Technologies says till the second quarter of 2013, the number of Internet connections having more than 4 Mbps speed in India was 2.1 per cent and those with more than 10 Mbps was barely 0.2 per cent.

And here's the sublime irony for a nation which prides on embracing a tech-enabled-change-driven future—the average connection speed in India is 1.3 Mbps. This is higher by 23 per cent in 2013 than in 2012 but the country still slips five positions in the ranking to 119 among 180 nations and continues

The average connection speed in India is 1.3 Mbps

to have the lowest connection speed in any Asian country reviewed.

The global average connection speed is 3.3 Mbps. South Korea has the highest average speed of 13.3 Mbps.

We are also down in the dumps in average peak connection speed where we rank 112th (having fallen three positions) and with a speed of 10.5 Mbps. Compare this with the best in the world: Hong Kong has an average peak connection speed of 65.1 Mbps and the global average is 18.9 Mbps.

Basically this is a bit like our demographic dividend. We keep talking about how it will change the country but in terms of providing infrastructure to use that dividend, we fail miserably.

66. Un-ready

The World Economic Forum's Global Information Technology Report 2013 ranks India at 68th position on its list of 144 countries surveyed to check 'networked readiness'.

What is 'networked readiness'? Here's how the report explains it: 'When The Global Information Technology Report (GITR) and the Networked Readiness Index (NRI) were created some 12 years ago, the attention of decision makers and investors was on adopting business and financial strategies that would allow them to develop in the context of a fast-moving but nascent Internet economy. Over more than a decade, the NRI has provided decision makers with a useful conceptual framework to evaluate the impact of information and communication technologies (ICTs) at a global level, and to benchmark the ICT readiness and the usage of their economies.'

Basically, is a country ready to engage with a technology driven, networked world?

In this we are behind countries like Malta, Slovenia, Latvia, Kazakhstan and Azerbaijan among many others.

67. Low Human Capital

Of 122 countries ranked on the global Human Capital Index, which is a measure of the economic potential of its labour force, India ranks 78th.

Oh, there goes our young population dividend then.

The Human Capital Index is a new tool to measure the long term potential of a country's work force. With the sad state of India's health, sanitation and hygiene, and terrible gender inequality, India ranks lower than China (43rd), Russia (51st) and Brazil (57th)—or lower than three of its four BRICS economies partners—and only South Africa at 86th is lower than India.

In the subdivision of the ranking, India was placed at the 49th place in workforce and employment, which means people are getting jobs and there are people who might want those jobs, but 63rd in education, 67th in an enabling environment and 112th in health and wellness.

Which means mostly the worker might not be equipped by circumstances to really do the jobs effectively, and why are we not surprised?

The top 10 countries in this list were Switzerland, Finland, Singapore, Netherlands, Sweden, Germany, Norway, the UK, Denmark and Canada.

68. I is for?

India lost ground in 2013 in the Global Innovation Index to 66th of 142 countries. Three countries in the BRICS partners—China, Brazil and Russia—are ahead of India.

The index measures institutions, human capital and research, infrastructure, market sophistication, business sophistication, knowledge and technology outputs and creative inputs. It takes into account everything from political stability to teacher-student ratio in school, to Wikipedia monthly edits to monthly uploads on You Tube.

Switzerland tops the survey done by the business school INSEAD, Cornell University and the World Intellectual Property Organisation.

Once again which are the kinds of countries innovating more than India? Not just Scandinavia and America, but also countries like Bosnia-Herzegovina (65th), Armenia (59th), Malta (24th), Estonia (25th), Slovkia (36th).

69. Pending Patents

In 2011, China beat the US to become the country filing the most number of patents in the world. This, says data from the World Intellectual Property Indicators.

The patent office in China received 526,412 applications in 2011 which was more than the US which had 503,582 applications. Of the top 20 countries in the world, India was at seventh place with 42,291 patent applications.

And here's what really cuts—China has increased its share of global patents filed from 37.2 per cent in 1995-2009 to 72.1 per cent in 2009–2011 whereas India's share fell from 3.5 per cent in 1995-2009 to 2.7 per cent in 2009–2011.

70. The Worst Place To Be A Woman

Among the wealthy G20 countries, India was voted as the worst place for a woman in 2013. TrustLaw, a legal news service of the Thomson Reuters Foundation, said that its survey of 370 gender specialists from around the world had placed India even below Saudi Arabia where women still can't drive and started voting only in 2011.

Canada topped the list, followed by Germany, Britain, Australia and France.

It pointed out all reasons India is the worst place for women—dowry murders, female foeticide and infanticide, or the murder of children before or after their birth because they are girls, relentless daily abuse, molestation and rape across India and some of the most unsafe and violent public spaces for women anywhere in the world, and constant discrimination.

Every BRICS nation was ahead of India—Brazil at 11, Russia at 13, China (15) and South Africa (17). Even Indonesia was ahead at 18.

71. The Steel Frame Pokes Hard!

The Indian bureaucracy was once the steel frame of the Raj. In 2012, the Political and Economic Risk Consultancy said that India had the worst and most inefficient bureaucracy in the world.

The Hong Kong-based consultancy ranked, between 1 and 10 (10 being the worst score), bureaucracies across Asia.

India scored 9.21 beating Vietnam, Indonesia, Philippines and China to the bottom spot.

Among other things, the report spoke of the complete lack of accountability of the average Indian bureaucrat and said, 'This gives them (bureaucrats) terrific powers and could be one of the main reasons average Indians, as well as existing and would-be foreign investors, perceive India's bureaucrats as negatively as they do.'

Singapore had the best performing bureaucracy with a rating of 2.25, followed by Hong Kong, Thailand, Japan, South Korea and Malaysia.

72. Not At Peace In India

The land of Gandhi is today ranked below the likes of Rwanda, Mynamar and Niger in the Global Peace Index.

Created by the Institute of Economics and Peace, the rankings put India at the 141st spot among 162 countries.

Some countries that are more peaceful than India—

- Sri Lanka (110)
- Republic of Congo (107)
- Haiti (92)
- Bangladesh (105)
- Uganda (106).

Among BRICS countries, India has a lower ranking than China (101), Brazil (81), South Africa (121). Only Russia is lower than India at 155 but then Russia is listed among the 10 most violent places in the world.

In South Asia, every country is ahead of India—Bhutan (20), Nepal (82), Bangladesh (105) and Sri Lanka (110) as mentioned above—expect Pakistan at 157 and Afghanistan.

India ranks 141 among 162 countries in the Global Peace Index

But both Pakistan and Afghanistan are among the 10 most dangerous places in the world on this list, along with the likes of Syria, Iraq, Somalia, North Korea, Democratic Republic of Congo and the Central African Republic.

73. Worst Airports in the World

Guess which airports pop up in the lists of the world's worst and the worst in Asia?

The Calcutta airport—ranked at the third spot in the top 10 worst airports in the world, by sleepinginairports.net in 2013 as voted by users and passengers at these airports.

At No 6 was Chennai and at No 8 was Mumbai. Just to note, Islamabad airport was voted better than Calcutta. And having been to both several times, I agree with this rating. The Islamabad airport is much better than the mad mess that is the Calcutta airport, even after its much flaunted revamp.

In the list of worst airports in Asia, we do even better!

Calcutta is the No 2 worst airport in Asia (again ahead of Islamabad), Chennai is at No 4, Mumbai is at No 5, and at No 10, a new worst airport entry from India—Bengaluru.

74. Also One of the World's Worst Airlines

Good old Air India is now a global leader. It is the world's third most unsafe airline after China Airlines and TAM Airlines.

This is a rating released in 2013 by the Hamburg-based Jet Airliner Crash Data Evaluation Centre (JACDEC).

Air India was ranked 58th of 60 airlines rated by JACDEC. Finnair was voted the world's safest airline, followed by Air New Zealand, Cathay Pacific and Emirates. The ratings are calculated every year using data on aircraft loss accidents and serious incidents over the previous 30 years.

The good news is that we have a truly world class new terminal in Mumbai which should take some of the pressure off the city airline traffic.

75. Worst Workplace

In 2013, the Bloomberg Businessweek magazine and the New York human resources company, ORC Worldwide, listed what they called the toughest places to work, the hardest postings in the globe.

At No 5 was Mumbai, described as a 'high risk location' with major problems of 'pollution, disease and sanitation, infrastructure and political violence', followed by New Delhi at No 6, pretty much for the same reasons.

At No 10 is Chennai, which has, the survey suggests, many of the issues of Delhi and Mumbai and a climate that is pretty much like the Delhi summer all year through!

The underlying theme of the survey about Indian cities—a shameful 3 among the top 10 worst places to work in the world—brings to light an old sin: that India has some of the worst public infrastructure in the world.

As we have mentioned before in this book, only the lord knows why Mumbai cannot get its corrupt politicians and builders to clean up their act and at least build all-weather roads.

76. We Don't Trust You

Never before have Indians trusted their own government as little as they trust it today. So says The Global Competitiveness Report of the World Economic Forum (WEF) in 2013.

India ranked 115 among 148 countries, an all-time low. In fact Indians (score 2.2) trust their politicians even less than the Pakistanis who ranked 110.

India also ranked lowest in this measure among all BRICS nations except Brazil (at 1.9), ranked at 136.

The measure of the chart was 1 = very low trust on politicians and 7 meant very high. Singapore rated the highest with a score of 6.2.

Since 2010, India has fallen by 27 spots on this ranking. In 2010, Pakistan was behind India but had now surpassed it. India also ranked 94th in government officials playing favourites and 98th in diversion of public funds.

77. Honour and Pride

The international Honour Based Violence Awareness Network says, each year around 1,000 honour killings happen in India, the same number as in Pakistan.

Naturally, most of those killed are women since our great 'tradition and culture' says honour is bound for some reason largely, if not only, with women.

The National Commission for Women in India says that it investigates 70-80 likely cases of honour killings every month.

In one of the most gruesome cases ever in 2012, a 29-year-old Muslim man cut off the head of his 22-year-old sister and brought it to the police station to surrender for murder. His relatives praised him for upholding their honour.

78. Our Slaves, Their Slaves

India ranked 4th among 162 countries for having some of the worst rates of modern-day slavery in the world—we have 13,956,010 (or nearly 14 million people) said the Global Slavery Index of the Australia-based Walk Free Foundation.

This is nearly half of the world's total number.

And the reasons for these include bonded labour, child labour, caste based exploitation, forced domestic labour and many more.

The countries above India—in the assessment of 'slave labour' to population—are Pakistan, Haiti and Mauritania.

79. Growing Old in India?

Basically don't. The Global Age Watch Index 2013 places India at No 73 in a list of 91 countries.

The only BRICS country India was ahead of was Russia (78). Brazil was at 31, China at 35 and South Africa at 65.

This was the first survey of its kind to gather data on how well the elderly were doing in a world which was ageing, and was put together by the Helpage International, the UN Population Fund and the World Health Organisation. It compares incomes, health, education, employment and ecosystems of the aged across the world.

The list was topped by Sweden.

80. Idle Money for the Labouring Worker

India has 45 million construction workers. Only 23 per cent of them are registered with welfare boards anywhere in the country.

The government has collected around Rs 9,300 crore as cess for workers welfare but, as it so often happens in the government, only 13 per cent of this money has been utilized. Where does this cess come from? It comes from the construction companies who are charged at around 1–2 per cent of the construction project size.

So why does this money not reach the workers?

Some light on this comes from issues in Haryana—where right to information questions found that only around three per cent of the labour cess had been used. But why? One of the reasons is that only workers registered with labour departments for about three to five years were entitled to get benefits.

Ask yourselves who are the people who work in construction around India? The answer is simple: migrants. Migrants from the poorer states like Bihar or Odisha. These are workers who travel between construction sites and their homes in the villages. They rarely have formalized contracts and usually no registration with labour departments.

These workers are the third largest kind of employees in the country and get zero job security and very little insurance, if any.

They are in jobs that are high risk and potentially dangerous at every moment, where one misstep can be fatal. Usually—unlike in every civilized country—they work without protective gear, mostly barely even footwear, not even a proper slipper sometimes, and often bare bodied. Yet, thousands of crore collected in their name are not provided for their welfare.

81. The Global Hub of Fake Resumes

In India, one in every 10 employee gives false information on their resume.

First Advantage, a technology company specializing in verifying resumes, has come out with this data and says employees fake everything from pay to previous job titles to tenure in past work.

The country has around 8,000 companies that help employees create forged resumes and sell fake work certificates.

82. What's in Your Food?

India's ministry of health and family welfare recently tested 29,328 samples of food, packaged, processed and loose, across 123 laboratories across the country.

They found that 20 per cent of all the food you and I eat—in every category from milk to cereals—were either adulterated or of substandard quality. These don't meet the quality standards of the Food Safety and Standards Authority of India.

And the shocking thing is that the amount of adulterated food in the market is rising. In 2008–09, amount of adulterated food was 8 per cent which has climbed to the 20 per cent in 2012–13.

83. The Criminals Among Us

Peek into the numbers of the National Crime Records Bureau and here's what you find: over the last 14 years, 20,452 people escaped from prison or police custody. Between 1999 and 2012, 4,136 people have escaped from police lock-ups while 16,316 people have escaped from police custody, outside lock-ups.

15,043 of these have been re-arrested. In these 14 years, 4,905 criminals who escaped from lock-ups have been re-arrested and 10,138 criminals who escaped from police custody, outside lock-ups have been re-arrested.

This means 5,409 criminals are out on the run and out somewhere, who knows perhaps near us?

84. At Home With Guns

Forty million Indians own guns, says gunpolicy.org, which tracks firearm policy and ownership across the world.

How many of these are registered? Barely 15 per cent. Which means 85 per cent of Indians who own guns have never registered them.

India has 3.36 private firearms to every 100 of population. This rate puts us at No. 110 at 178 countries in rate of firearms per hundred of population.

The bad news is that in a country as large as India, this still means we have enough privately held guns to put us at No 2 of 178 countries in sheer numbers of civilian owned guns.

Ninety per cent of murders in India are committed using these private weapons.

And while Pakistan, a far more violent society than India, has more guns per hundred people (more than 11), in total it has less than half the civilian guns as India—only 18 million.

85. Shooting the Messenger

In the first six months of 2013, India was the second most dangerous place in the world for those working in the business of news.

The first was Syria, which is in the middle of a massive civil war between the government forces of Bashar al-Assad and rebels.

The London-based International News Safety Institute counted eight journalists dead in Syria during this period, while six were killed in India.

Let us look at how and why they were killed.

Nemi Chand Jain, a journalist from Chhattisgarh, had his throat slit and a note left on him, which accused him of being a police informer. Local criminals and the police are said to be behind the murder.

Three employees of a Bengali newspaper—a proof reader, the manager of the newspaper and a driver—were murdered. Later the editor of the newspaper said that he was the target and instead these people were killed.

Two other journalists were killed in accidents.

Even if we discount the last two, in four cases people working in news were directly targeted and murdered. That would put India at the same level as Somalia—at number four—where four journalists were killed during the same time, and just below Pakistan where five died.

This is not the first time India has been one of the worst places in the world to be a journalist. We were among the top five even in 2010.

86. Badly Behaved in the World

We cut queues. We shove. We spit. We pee in public if we can. We ogle at women. If we get a chance, and see that we can get away, we sometimes grope.

We tip badly, if at all. We are sloppy dressers. We complain loudly, and insist on speaking in our own tongue in front of people who don't understand the language. We scream on the mobile phone in public.

We have iffy personal hygiene. There are some of us who dig our noses during a long haul flight and stick their fingers into the ear and waggle furiously.

And therefore we are at No 7 in top 10 list of the Business Insider website of the world's worst tourists.

China is at No 1. (Happy?)

Basically we treat our tourists badly when they come to our country and behave terribly ourselves when we go out into the world.

What does it say about us as a people? And how can India truly be Incredible India—in spite of all the marketing—like this?

87. Fraud on the Inside

A majority of Indian companies are affected by fraud, says a report of the Economic Intelligence Unit and the US risk consultancy, Kroll.

This fraud costs these companies at an average 1.4 per cent of their revenues. The report came after Kroll researchers spoke to 900 senior executives around the world to make the annual Global Fraud Report.

They found that in India, 24 per cent of the companies had lost revenues through bribery and corruption,(which is a good 10 per cent above the world average) and 22 per cent had lost money via internal financial fraud, far ahead of the global average of 16 per cent.

Most people, or 89 per cent, said the fraud was done by an insider and 29 per cent said frauds happened because of the frequency with which employees left and joined work.

88. Escape the Tax Man

Each year India loses around Rs 14 trillion in taxes due to evasion, which is equal to around \$226 billion—this is the assessment of Arun Kumar, who wrote the book *The Black Economy of India*. Just to get a sense of how much this is, India's foreign currency reserves, as of October 2013, were around \$281 billion.

India gets only 15.5 per cent of GDP from taxes, which is one of the lowest tax bases among G20 countries says the Centre for Budget and Governance Accountability. Only two countries are lower; Mexico (14.5) and Indonesia (10.89).

Our share of direct taxes to total taxes is 37.7 per cent, much less than countries like South Africa at 57.5 per cent, Russia (41.3 per cent) and Indonesia at 55.85 per cent.

The property tax-to-GDP ratio in India is only 0.48 per cent; for France and the UK, it is 4.3 per cent and 4.21 per cent, respectively. For China, it is 1.73 per cent. Wealth tax in India is only 0.007 per cent of GDP, while it is 0.89 per cent in France.

There are only 1.5 crore direct tax payers in the country

The income tax department estimates that half of India's

around 3.4 crore income tax payers pay less than or around Rs 1,000! So for all practical purposes there are only 1.5 crore direct tax payers in the country.

89. The Poor Declared Crorepati

The economic joke of the decade is perhaps Finance Minister P. Chidambaram's declaration that there are only 42,000 crorepatis in India.

What he meant of course was that only 42,000 people declare an income for Rs 1 crore or more a year.

The rest? Well, that's a different story, one that you and I know quite well.

90. When in Doubt, Smuggle

In 2013, faced with troubling financials and a falling rupee, the government raised duties on the import of gold. Guess what happened?

Between April and September 2013, more gold was caught being smuggled in (four time more to be precise) than in the same quarter of 2012.

As this book was being written, the estimates were that more gold would be caught being smuggled in this year than in the past 10 years. How much more? Around 50 per cent more.

Think about that—in a country where malnutrition and hunger is chronic such is the lust for gold that we are willing to break any law, do anything to get gold.

Between 2003 and 2013, gold worth Rs 199 crore was seized by customs. In 2013-14, the amount was likely to be around Rs 250–300 crore.

Now, here's something else to think about—only about 5 to 10 per cent of the gold being smuggled in is actually caught. Think about the amount and value of gold actually being smuggled in.

It's worth thinking whether government strategy really worked here—and also about why we lust for gold so much as a society.

91. Black is the Colour of Money

In 2012, India or Indians had 2.18 billion Swiss francs in Swiss banks.

In 2013, this dipped to 1.42 billion Swiss francs or around Rs 9,000 crore.

Oh, we see, now that must be the reason India dropped five spots on the annual global Prosperity Index of the London-based Legatum Institute. In 2013, we were at 101—in the 2014 index we fell below even Bangladesh to 106th place among 142 countries. Among the things that the Legatum Institute measures are all those ideas that we have never been good at—education, health, economy, safety, security.

The financial researcher Global Financial Integrity says that in 2011, over Rs 4 lakh crore worth of black money was illegally taken out of India—24 per cent more than in 2010.

This is around one third of the Indian government's budgeted expenditure in 2011, 14 times what was spent on health, seven times what was spent on education and five times the amount spent on rural development.

92. Retail Theft

The Global Retail Theft Barometer in 2011 said that for five straight years, customers from one country had been the world's biggest thieves from shops.

Indians.

The term the retail industry uses for this shoplifting is shrink rate—literally the rate at which their stocks shrink—and this is due to stealing by customers, employees and suppliers. India had the highest shrink rate of 2.38 per cent which amounted to losses to Rs 3,470 to local stores.

The study was done by the Centre for Retail Research in Nottingham in the UK and covered 43 countries and 1,187 retailers. In India, 100 retailers were surveyed including 60 from modern chains and 40 that belonged to the unorganised sector.

What do people steal the most? Clothes, for one. Grocery, easy to hide, easy to flick. Also health and beauty products like shaving products and perfumes.

India had company at the top of the shrink rate from Russia and Morocco while the lowest shrink rates, or the most honest shoppers, were to be found in Japan, Hong Kong and Taiwan.

So who's doing all the stealing? Mostly customers it seems (or 47.6 per cent) followed by employees (25.5 per cent).

The good news is that we had stolen less by 12.5 per cent in 2011 than in 2010.

93. An Arm and a Leg for an Ambassador

How many diplomats does the country that wants to be a permanent member of the United Nations Security Council need?

If it is India, it seems one makes do with—now what's the exact number? Even there, there seems to be some confusion. The Ministry of External Affairs' own website says, 'In recent years, the intake into the Indian Foreign Service has averaged between 8-15 persons annually. The present cadre strength of the service stands at approximately 600 officers manning around 162 Indian missions and posts abroad and the various posts in the Ministry at home.'

Other reports suggest that with recent inductions, the strength has gone up to—depending on which report you are reading—between 845 and 930.

Now let's look at the key Security Council members. How many does the US have? 20,000. China? 6,200. France? 6,000. Even Brazil has more than twice as many diplomats as India.

Clearly not the strength an emerging power usually shows in engaging the world.

94. Out-bid and Outsmarted by... who else...China

In 2013, India's *navratna* energy company, ONGC (Oil and Natural Gas Corporation), lost a major Kazakhstan oilfield to the Chinese.

ONGC had tried for an 8.4 per cent stake in the oilfield owned by America's ConocoPhillips for $5 billion until the Kazakh's decided to use their right to first refusal clause and buy back the stake, only to sell it to China's China National Petroleum Corp (CNPC) for around $5.3 billion.

This is just the latest round that the country has lost to China as the Asian giants roam the world in search of resources to secure the future of their billions of people. In 2010, ONGC was beaten in the race to acquire Ugandan oilfields by China's CNOOC (China National Offshore Oil Corporation).

In 2005, CNPC piped ONGC to the post by buying PetroKazakhstan for $4.18 billion. Also that year, CNPC beat ONGC to buy Ecuador's Encana Corp for $1.42 billion. In 2011, ONGC failed to pick up Exxon Mobil Corp's share in an Angolan oil field.

Bloomberg data shows in the last five years, Indian companies have made oil and gas acquisitions around the world worth $13.6 billion while the Chinese have spent 9 times that at $107 billion.

India's rare success against the Chinese has been in working recently with Royal Dutch Shell to keep away China's Sinochem from a Brazilian oilfield.

In Myanmar, India faces an even more humiliating situation. ONGC Videsh and Gas Authority of India Ltd (GAIL) have a stake in two gas blocks in the country. But they couldn't manage to convince the Naypyidaw government to sell the gas to India. Instead, the Chinese convinced the Myanmar government to sell them the gas at a cheaper rate than what India pays for international gas.

95. India Vs China

This is the assessment by the Global Fire Power site that analyses defence preparedness between countries of the comparative positions of India and China:

Active Military Personnel
India—1,325,000
China—2,285,000

Active Military Reserves
India—1,747,000
China—800,000

Total Aircraft Strength
India—1,962
China—5,048

Total Helicopter Strength
India—620
China—901

Total Tank Strength
India—3,555
China—7,950

Total Armoured Fighting Vehicle Strength
India—2,293
China—18,700

Total Self Propelled Gun Strength
India—330
China—2,500

Towed Artillery Strength
India—6,585
China—25,000

Total Multiple Launch Rocket Strength
India—292
China—2,600

Total Mortar Strength
India—5,000
China—10,050

Anti-Tank Weaponry Strength
India—51,800
China—31,250

Logistical Vehicle Strength
India—70,000
China—75,850

Merchant Marine Strength
India—340
China—2,032

Major Ports and Terminals
India—7
China—8

Total Navy Ship Strength
India—170
China—972

Aircraft Carrier Strength
India—1
China—1

Submarine Fleet Strength
India—15
China—63

Frigate Strength
India—14
China—47

Destroyer Strength
India—8
China—25

Corvette Strength
India—24
China—0

Mine Warfare Craft Strength
India—8
China—52

Coastal Patrol Craft Strength
India—31
China—322

Amphibious Assault Craft Strength
India—16
China—228

Last year, when India celebrated the launch of its first long range intercontinental ballistic missile Agni-V which has a range of more than 5,000 kilometres and up to Beijing, the Chinese response was largely dismissive since its own Dongfeng 5A missiles have a range of 13,000 kilometres. China, an integral part of the club of nations that have long range ballistic missiles capable of carrying nuclear warheads which includes the US, Britain, Russia and France, also has 66 land-based intercontinental missile launchers. India has none.

In 2008, Chinese soldiers 'lost their way in Indian territory' 270 times. In the last 12 months, there have been numerous Chinese incursions into India including in Ladakh. India is creating a special 50,000-strong mountain corps, spending an estimated $11 billion to defend its border positions with China but that will take at least six years to come into action.

96. No More Ceasefire

India's decade old ceasefire on the border with Pakistan lies shattered.

The Indian Army says at least 200 violations of the ceasefire agreement of 2003 has been made from the Pakistani side during the course of 2013.

And on one occasion in October 2013, around 50 of its border posts were shelled. In a sense, the gloves are off once again.

97. How Does the Government's Best Known Scheme Work?

One way to get a peek into how our government works is to see what the auditor Comptroller and Auditor General (CAG) of India had to say when it audited the Mahatma Gandhi National Rural Employment Guarantee Act, our most expensive government scheme costing Rs 1,923,22.33 crore since its inception in 2005–06.

What did the CAG find? Let's look at four big things:

1. That 31 per cent of the gram panchayats (surveyed across 11 states) who are supposed to apply the scheme, had no real proper plans on how to use the money.
2. Also, excess funds of Rs 2374.86 crore were released to six states, either due to wrong calculations or without taking into account balances available in these states. Then, in 2010-11, the government released Rs 6,733.25 crore to states, without taking into account the unspent balances of Rs 10,104.71 crore as on 31st March 2010. Similarly, in 2011–12, Government of Indian (GOI) released Rs 2,440

crore to four states without taking into account unspent balances amounting to Rs 3758.91 crore.

3. Photographs of 4.33 lakh job cards (usually an important guard against fraud) were missing in seven states.
4. Bihar, Maharashtra and Uttar Pradesh, which together accounted for 46 per cent of the rural poor, utilised only 20 per cent of GOI funds. In contrast, Andhra Pradesh, Chhattisgarh, Rajasthan, Tamil Nadu and West Bengal utilised more funds as compared to their poverty levels.

So how is MNREGA working? It would be easy to immediately say that it isn't. Actually the truth has a huge lesson in the way we work, the way our country works, and why it is critical to discuss policy rather than *Feku* and *Pappu*.

Basically MNREGA shows that when it works, when the money is given to the people, when the work they do that it is important to the village community, and especially if the transfer is done through bank accounts, it can be an enriching, vital scheme. Quite like if PDS works, like it does in Chhattisgarh, it is empowering. But it needs that oft-used and abused phrase—political will—to make it happen.

98. The Economic Mind of the BJP

If there is one thing that is true for the polls in 2014, it is that this is going to be the big economic election in India. The rise of an aspiring class is, in many ways, shattering many certainties of the old welfare state. Make no mistake though—big social welfare schemes are not disappearing in a hurry but today the voters want more. The promise of a better life is increasingly more vital than the promise of free rice.

In this chapter and next we will look at—in brief—the basic economic agenda of the two main parties, the Congress and the BJP.

Atal Bihari Vajpayee, the famed former prime minister of India from the Bharatiya Janata Party, was fond of telling a story of his tiff with Jawaharlal Nehru, the first prime minister of the country.

In the mid-50s, Vajpayee was a young MP in a Parliament, overwhelmed by the Congress and led by the charismatic Nehru himself. There was a debate on building The Ashoka Hotel, which was to be India's first luxury hotel. In one of the debates, Vajpayee pointed out that the job of the government is to build hospitals, not hotels. Nehru, patrician and renowned for his erudition, was furious at the intrusion of a junior MP from a then virtually non-existent political party. He snapped at Vajpayee, saying that the young man didn't understand anything and that hospitals will be made from the profits of the hotel. Vajpayee used to joke that that hotel is still loss-making and you can see how many hospitals have been built.

This anecdote ought to emphatically emphasise the BJP's right of centre, pro-market, pro-business mind but it is actually not that simple. The BJP is, for all practical purposes, India's Right, only sometimes not quite.

But the BJP has always had a tussle on its economic soul. The founding father of the Bharatiya Jan Saṇgh, the precursor to BJP, Shyama Prasad Mookerjee, was a free market proponent. He was the industry minister in the cabinet of the first prime minister, Jawaharlal Nehru, and differed with Nehruvian socialism. Economic freedom, Mookerjee argued, is one of the four key planks of nation building, along with national, political and personal liberty. 'Freedom consists, not only in the absence of restraint, but also in the presence of opportunity,' he famously said on 27 November 1937, at the convocation of Patna University.

When Mookerjee fell out with Nehru and started the Jan Sangh in 1951, it naturally became a champion of the market. The twist here is that the Jan Sangh and Mookerjee were closely associated with their ideological parent, the nationalist Rashtriya Swayam Sewak Sangh (RSS), a strong advocate of swadeshi or homemade growth in every field—from Indian culture and clothing to Indian companies. The slogan for this homegrown-ism was given by the other stalwart of the Jan Sangh movement, the social reformer Deen Dayal Upadhayay, who spoke of antyodaya or caring for the poorest of the poor, a takeoff from Mahatma Gandhi's famous advice—'Recall the face of the poorest and weakest man you have seen and ask yourself if this step you contemplate is going to be of any use to him'.

This has given economic thinking within the BJP, a history of confusion but political maneuverability to pick and choose which part of its history it wants to tap into at what point.

Atal Bihari Vajpayee, who left journalism to join politics, inspired by Mookerjee, clearly chose his mentor's path. As did the man who presented five budgets for him, Yashwant Sinha, the former finance minister.

But in September 2012, at a Stanford University lecture, Sinha spoke of how his commitment to market-friendly policy making had only brought him grief. He took blame for the BJP's epic rout in 2004. 'Sometimes, I feel that I may have been responsible single handedly for the defeat of my party in the 2004 elections. I can never forget the lessons I learnt in that election,' said Sinha.

'During my tenure as finance minister, I had raised the prices of kerosene oil from Rs 2.50 to Rs 9.50; kerosene oil is used on a large scale in the rural areas for both lighting as well as cooking. When I went campaigning in a remote village in my constituency, and asked an old woman for her vote, she said that that was fine, but was I not responsible for raising oil prices which had made her life difficult?'

Even arguably BJP's topmost contribution to India's development—building new highways—didn't help it win the 2004 elections. BJP and its allies lost all 14 seats which it had won in 1998 along the arterial

'When I went campaigning in a remote village in my constituency, and asked an old woman for her vote, she said that that was fine, but was I not responsible for raising oil prices which had made her life difficult?'

National Highway 2, connecting eastern and north western India.

So it was Nitin Gadkari, who became BJP president in 2009 after the party had lost two elections in a row, who brought in the antyodaya as the motto in part, to counter two Congress mantras aimed at the poorest—the Congress ka Haath Aam Aadmi ke saath (the hand of the Congress is with the common man) which trumped the BJP's India Shining in 2004 and Mahatma Gandhi National Employment Guarantee Act which promised at least 100 days manual labour for the rural poor.

But that was just the centre in Delhi. The core of BJP's thought making was already shifting.

To try and understand the economic mind of the Bharatiya Janata Party (BJP), I took a ruler, a scale if you will, and drew parallel lines through the heart of India. The states that fall between these lines are Gujarat, Madhya Pradesh and Chattisgarh.

They are what the BJP describes as their 'model states'. They are also some of the fastest growing states in India. Each of these states show off different aspects of the economic mind of the BJP—Gujarat shows over all ability to fix many of the problems that plague India (power theft, urban squalor, creating business friendly environments), Madhya Pradesh, led by Chief Minister Shivraj Singh Chouhan, has been about the spectacular turnaround of a sinking, ramshackle state into the agricultural powerhouse clocking an 18 per cent growth in wheat production in 2011–12, beating traditional agrarian giants like Punjab and Haryana and winning the annual award for best performance in agriculture for the year.

Chhattisgarh, under Raman Singh, which was created as a new state at the same time as Jharkhand, had Rs 49 more as per capita income than Jharkhand in 2004–05, but in 2012 the gap had widened to Rs 6,733. In a state plagued with Naxal violence,

Chhattisgarh still managed to transform one of the biggest problem areas of governance—the theft-ridden, corruption plagued public distribution system through which subsidized food is provided to the poor.

Just by plugging the holes (theft in many parts of the country are as high as 40 per cent of the food supplied) and bringing it down to under 5 per cent, Chhattisgarh managed to bring down malnutrition from 54 per cent in 2006 to 38 per cent six years later.

Both Shivraj Singh Chouhan and Raman Singh have now won a third term.

And as is becoming increasingly evident, it's the states that are beginning to influence BJP's economic thinking.

This is the key difference between the Congress and the BJP today. In the Congress, power still trickles down from party president Sonia Gandhi and son Rahul. In the forthcoming elections, the economic outlook of the Congress will be shaped by leaders like P. Chidambaram, Jairam Ramesh, Kamal Nath, Salman Khurshid and Kapil Sibal, each primarily a part of the Delhi-based central leadership.

This is not to say that there will not be inputs from central leaders. Sinha says, if given a chance again, there are four things that'll top his agenda—bring down the number of central government-funded schemes from the current 147 to 10, have these schemes fully financed by the centre and do away with the current method of joint financing with the states, and have stringent monitoring of the schemes. 'At the moment, around 100 schemes have a budget of less than Rs 300 crore. What we would apply are 10 really big ticket schemes in the areas of infrastructure, power, health and agriculture which will be on the basis of demand from the states, a bottom-up approach, instead of top down,' he says.

Both Sinha and Arun Shourie also worry about the ballooning fiscal deficit and Sinha's formula to reduce the deficit to less than 3 per cent, hinges on what he calls 'immediately implementable planning'. He suggests dismantling the current system of five year plans envisaged by the central Planning Commission and reducing its term to two years to be able to focus on what can be implemented quickly. The idea of a Planning Commission with five-year terms was borrowed from the Soviets and dates to Jawaharlal Nehru's first prime-ministerial term.

Shourie says he despairs at the use of monetary policy to curb inflation, which he says is like 'using an axe to kill a mosquito'. 'We are in this vicious cycle. Neglect inflation, fiscal deficit spins out of control, and we respond through increased interest rates. We have off-budget expenses each year of around Rs 200,000 crore (in fuel and fertiliser subsidies) and no one talks about that,' says Shourie, who proposes a complete freeze on all hikes on government expenditure except in defence and internal security. 'We must restrict the use of monetary policy and focus on fiscal policy. The focus must be on efficient delivery.'

Both Sinha and Shourie are also arguing against the Gadgill-Mukherjee formula of distribution of central funds to states. Created in 1990 by social scientist D. R. Gadgill and Pranab Mukherjee, the incumbent president who was then deputy chairman, planning commission, as per the formula, of every Rs 100 sent to the states, 55 per cent is on the basis of population (larger the population, more assistance), 25 per cent on the basis of per capita income, 5 per cent on fiscal management and 15 per cent on special problems including disasters, crumbling urban spaces, etc. Shourie and Sinha argue that post liberalisation, with states often taking their own economic destiny in their hands, the formula is irrelevant.

The influence of the states is all but visible in this thinking.

Six years back, Narendra Modi had already begun railing against the Gadgill-Mukherjee formula. He called it a formula that 'punished' fiscally responsible, innovative and aggressively growing states. As a solution, he suggested that each state be allowed to submit three critical areas for assistance, instead of the centre judging needs and allocating budgets accordingly. With a Congress government at the centre, predictably Modi's suggestions were dismissed, but if the BJP wins, expect the Gadgill-Mukherjee formula to be re-crafted, if not scrapped outright. This will enable states to get a far greater control on their fiscal targets because demand for money will come from the states depending on their priority areas like health or education rather than population or per capita income.

Even on curbing fiscal deficit, the BJP knows that its states can show the way. According to a report by the PHD Chamber of Commerce in July 2012, most of the heartland BJP states had reigned in their deficit at less than 3 per cent. The report listed Chhattisgarh as 'excellent' with a deficit of 1.9 per cent of the state GDP, while Madhya Pradesh and Gujarat were dubbed 'very good' at 3 per cent.

Even in this, note the whiff of the states: Madhya Pradesh has already started increasing the procurement price of wheat leading to bumper crops. In Madhya Pradesh, Chief Minister Chouhan has offered a revolutionary farmer loan at 1 per cent scheme and an extra Rs 100 per quintal to the central government procurement price. Earlier in 2012, Chouhan explained the core of economic thought to me as 'firm focus on agriculture and fulfilling the needs of the poorest'. Like Modi, he also has a successful scheme in providing free ambulance service to low-income pregnant women to boost girl child births in the state. But in a sense, Modi and Chouhan represents the two biggest influences on economic thought within the BJP—Modi in the legacy of Shyama Prasad Mookerjee and Chouhan from Deen Dayal Upadhayay.

The final radical pillar of BJP economics these days is Subramanian Swamy. Swamy says he is pro-FDI in retail but with strings attached. 'I believe in parity,' says Swamy. 'I am happy to welcome in, say Walmart, if the US allows Indians workers to go work in their infrastructure in their country. Otherwise why should their low cost capital be applied in India to earn profit while India's surplus labour cannot earn from their country?' Basically this means he is against FDI in retail, at least for all practical purposes.

Swamy, whose early mentors and inspirations were Simon Kuznets, Paul Samuelson and Milton Friedman, have brought what can be called the idea of nationalist capitalism to the Jan Sangh in the 70s—a free market swadeshi, if you will. It was based on economic liberalism, complete breakaway from Nehruvian socialism and focuses on building Indian infrastructure and enterprises, including increased focus on agriculture. Even today he says linking Indian rivers—one of former prime minister Atal Bihari Vajpayee's pet projects—and extensive irrigation for agriculture are the two projects closest to his heart. 'We have forgotten the art of self sufficiency,' he says.

'I am happy to welcome in, say Walmart, if the US allows Indian workers to go work in their infrastructure in their country.'

The BJP's prime ministerial candidate Narendra Modi has now given us a vision of an era of continuous construction, as it were, from bringing bullet trains to building 100 new cities—but the big question is where is the land and the money going to come from?

BJP's ideology can be called free market nationalism—it believes in the free market, but only if it helps in the case of nation building. Will it work? We shall see.

99. The Economic Mind of the Congress (and More Specifically of Rahul Gandhi)

In December 2012, Rahul Gandhi made a vital economic statement. He told a meeting of party chiefs from 51 districts, where cash transfers were being rolled out, that the scheme would keep the party in power for at least 10 years.

Exactly around one year later, the Congress saw two of its worst electoral defeats ever in two of the states where cash transfers were piloted—namely Rajasthan and Madhya Pradesh.

So what is happening?

Basically the Congress' economics is based on an idea of providing welfare to the poor. And that worked for them for a very long time. In fact, conventional wisdom says that the Mahatma Gandhi National Rural Employment Guarantee Scheme and the farm loan waiver helped the Congress notch a big victory in 2009.

But in the meantime, something changed.

Aspirations became more important and simultaneously deliverance of giant welfare schemes failed to improve. For instance in Rajasthan, where the Congress launched myriad social schemes under the Ashok Gehlot government—including free medical care and pension plans for the elderly and physically disabled—the BJP won a landslide victory.

I started tracking Congress' economic thinking, indeed Rahul Gandhi's economic thinking, three years ago when I joined Fortune's India offices and long before he spoke of India as a busy beehive to the Confederation of Indian Industry (CII) in April 2013.

If you read Rahul Gandhi's beehive speech carefully, there is a subtext that emerges. The subtext is lack of trust in politics (his other big speech in January 2013 in Jaipur talked about how power can be poisonous) but there was also an economic subtext that has barely been discussed.

It could well be that this was one of the most important economic speeches in recent times. Why? Note that Rahul Gandhi is not new in talking about beehives to discuss human morals and economies. In 1714, the Dutch philosopher, political economist and satirist Bernard Mandeville wrote a poem called *The Fable of the Bees* where he described many principles that would later inspire Adam Smith and John Maynard Keynes. For instance, the idea of private vices and public virtue; that a greater common good comes from consumption and not saving and that perfect moral virtue is perhaps unattainable and undesirable for modern nation states; and that a division of labour is inherently necessary for growth and prosperity.

Rahul Gandhi is clever enough to see that his party runs a deeply corrupt government, which itself is a by-product of a deeper rot in Indian society. But in a sense he is arguing, like Mandeville, that it is only a state with clear laws and punishment that can hold peace in a nation and not lofty ideals of virtue. That's the soto voce point he tried to make in that fervent press conference after the losses in four states when he promised change.

Rahul Gandhi is clever enough to see that his party runs a deeply corrupt government, which itself is a by-product of a deeper rot in Indian society

I traced echoes of his father Rajeev Gandhi's economics in one of the first big economic interventions he made on behalf of the tribals of Niyamgiri in Odisha.

In 1989, in rural Maharashtra, his father said for the Bhil tribals, 'We know and you know that the forests were not spoiled for thousands of years. The tribals have never damaged the forests. Sometimes outsiders have misguided the tribals for their own benefit and oppressed them. Our effort is to rectify these wrongs.'

In 2010, for the Dongaria Kondhs, Rahul said: 'This is your hill. It is sacred to you. You have protected your hill. Some people said this is against development. This is not true. There is no development without the voice of the poor.'

The thing is—unlike his father who helped the Congress grow in Maharashtra—in Odisha, the Congress still remains a permanent challenger to the ruling Biju Janata Dal. What is happening to the Congress is that either the credit for its big schemes is usurped by the ruling party—like cash transfers was embraced by the Shivraj Singh Chouhan government and which also became its face in many places—or in states where it fights for local rights, its appeal does not somehow convert into votes.

It is not that the Congress always gets its economics wrong but it does seem to be unable to enthuse people about its economics; perhaps because the language of its economics lies deeply in language of handouts and not aspiration. There is clear evidence that its rights-based economics is creating a new aspiring consumer class but that class does not seem to be listening to the Congress pitch and seems to not be voting for the party. This is a curious situation for a party which ruled the first phase of India's independent life on Jawaharlal Nehru's socialist policies, followed by his daughter's stringent nationalism—but also was the party whose prime minister, Narasimha Rao, with his finance minister Manmohan Singh, opened the economy.

The irony for the Congress today is that the generation of liberalization, the children of the aspirations unleashed by that opening are turning away from the Congress—and in many cases, it is rivals like the BJP, who have appropriated the mantle of carrying forward the agenda of reforms rather than the Congress. Its single largest challenge is to keep the children of liberalization engaged to its politics and policies. What Rahul Gandhi lacks is a big imaginative economic idea. His great grandfather had the idea of building an independent India and his big dams which he called the temples of modern India. His grandmother had a forceful nationalism—including of banks—and the abolishing of privy purses of the royals and the slogan 'garibi hatao' or remove poverty. His father's big idea was to bring India into a computer-enabled age. Even his mother had her big ticket social schemes and the motto that won 2004 for her—'Congress ka haath aam aadmi ke saath'. But at a time when the aam aadmi itself even has a separate party to its name, what is Rahul Gandhi's big economic idea? What is his slogan?

What Rahul Gandhi lacks is a big imaginative economic idea

In recent times, Gandhi has been a vigorous proponent of the policies that seem closest to his mother's heart. The Food Security Bill for instance and the Land Acquisition law are both attempts to solve some of the worst inadequacies of India's growth over the last 20 years—why are so many people still hungry, why are farmers cheated of their land by providing subsidized food to two-thirds of Indians and raising price of land by up to four times—and yet, such is the deep rooted corruption within the Indian system that few believe that benefits would reach the beneficiaries without massive pilfer.

And therefore, perhaps it is not Gandhi's myriad long speeches but one of his shortest ones that give an insight into his economics—his dismissing the ordinance to keep convicted parliamentarians in their seat. Because without a vigorous clean up of his own party, none of his and his mother's best intentioned schemes will bear fruit.

For evidence of this we need to only look towards MNREGA to see how a scheme could be afflicted by corruption—though through direct cash transfers there might be some hope of reform—and deep inefficiencies.

As Gandhi looks for the right path to industrialisation, he's not going to be able to please everyone. His challenge is to figure out whom he can afford to please less or there is bound to be tension between business and Gandhi, in quite the same way as President Obama once seemed to be fighting industry.

In his maiden TV interview to Times Now, Rahul Gandhi promised to bring China-style manufacturing muscle to India and make it the global manufacturing hub. But the contradiction lies in the fact that one of the biggest challenges to that vision is the new tougher land acquisition law that his own government has passed. Does he not realize that China's manufacturing might is based on swift acquiring of millions of acres of land—and the displacement of millions of people—both of which the new law makes much, much tougher?

Rahul Gandhi's role finally might be to remind us as Mandeville did:

Bare Virtue can't make Nations live
In Splendor; they, that would revive
A Golden Age, must be as free,
For Acorns, as for Honesty.

100. Shit Politicians Say—and Some Good Men

In the end, here are some of the things that the people we have voted to power have said in recent days. As you read these comments, think about how you are going to vote in the future.

'From where we will give him water? Should we urinate in dams?'

– Ajit Pawar, Nationalist Congress Party during
the drought in Vidarbha

'Dented-painted women protesters in Delhi went to discotheques and then turned up at India Gate to express outrage.'

– Abhijit Mukherjee, Indian National Congress
after the Delhi gang rape case

'I don't feel any hesitation in saying that 90 per cent of the girls want to have sex intentionally but they don't know that they would be gang raped further as they find some lusty and pervasive people in the way ahead.'

– Dharambir Goyat, Indian National Congress
after the Delhi gang rape case

'Girl, sorry to say, you belong to CPI(M) cadre. SFI cadre you are...They are Maoists...'

– Mamata Banerjee, Trinamool Congress to a school student asking her questions on a TV show

'Who amongst us has not followed girls?'

– Sharad Yadav, Janata Dal (United) during the anti-rape bill debate in Parliament

'Women should not venture out with men who are not relatives.'

– Abu Azmi, Samajwadi Party

'We have no answer to this rising spate of crimes against women. Stars are not in position,'

– Nanki Ram Kanwar, Bharatiya Janata Party, talking about rising rape cases

But these are not the only politicians we have in India. There are some others too. Let's end with the example of a few who are rarely spoken of but in many ways define what a politician ought to be.

His name is Manik Sarkar and he is at the moment chief minister of Tripura for the fourth time and a member of the ruling Communist Party of India (Marxist) or CPI(M). He doesn't have a car. He owns no home. His wife travels in an auto. His declared assets barely touch Rs 2.5 lakh. He donates every penny of his chief minister's salary of Rs 12,500 a month to the party and gets a Rs 5,000 allowance from the CPI(M). Last heard, there was a proposal to raise the salary of the chief minister to Rs 18,750.

But he is not the only one. In Sikkim, which was voted the best place to visit in the world in 2014 by Lonely Planet, there is a man called Pawan Chamling, who has won four elections in a row. Between 2007 and 2012, his state grew at 9 per cent at an average every year, every village home in the state has electricity (as does every town home), and it is also the only state where there is no open defecation. It has booming businesses in hydro-electricity, tourism and pharmaceuticals.

Then there is Arvind Kejriwal and his Aam Aadmi Party. A party once dismissed as nothing. It won 28 seats in the Delhi Assembly elections and now says it has a presence in 300 districts across India.

You have been looking for change. Change is here. It is in that finger of yours. Yes, that one. Change is a black spot on your finger. It is a talisman, a *til* to guard against the evil eye. There are 100 things to think about before you vote. But you have only one vote.

As I finished writing this book, the Finance Minister, Palaniappan Chidambaram asked a gathering of India's biggest business leaders at an awards ceremony, 'Shall we barter the glorious idea of India for a few more kilometres of roads, for a few more kilo tonnes of coal, for a few more kilowatts of power?'

I see what the minister is trying to say—and he is not wrong in defending India's inclusiveness. But to me it also seemed that these questions should be asked to parents who see their children die because the ambulance does not reach on time, because the roads are bad, because the operation theatre barely exists, to children who cannot study because there is never any electricity, millions of those who have never had electricity since independence. To

'Shall we barter the glorious idea of India for a few more kilometres of roads, for a few more kilo tonnes of coal, for a few more kilowatts of power?'

me it seemed that when he spoke of the glorious idea of India, it was his glorious idea of India that he was thinking about, not ours.

To those who struggle desperately each day in a 21st century nation with 19th, even 18th century infrastructure, the minister's words might sound a bit like, 'Let them eat the glorious idea of India instead'.

Think. Vote.

Bibliography

Chapter 1

'India's poverty level falls to record 22%: Planning Commission', *Mint*, 23 July 2013

Chapter 3

'Each minute of Parliament in sessions costs Rs. 2.5 lakh', Press Trust of India (PTI), 7 September 2012

'Parliament's Winter Session: A Report Card', *The New York Times*, 24 December 2012

'Parliament monsoon session: some work done, a lot of time wasted', *Down To Earth*, 9 September 2013

'Shall we call the President?', *Tehelka*, 25 June 2011

Chapter 4

http://rajyasabha.nic.in/rsnew/members/entitlement_salary_mp.pdf

'Lok Sabha clears higher salaries for MPs', *The Times of India*, 28 August 2010

Chapter 5

Members page, Rajya Sabha, Parliament of India website: http://adrindia.org/research-and-reports/lok-sabha/2009/

full-asset-details-mps-lok-sabha-2009-election Association of Democratic Reforms

'Crorepati MPs double in LS, average assets tripled: ADR,' PTI, 22 November 2009

'No business like politics in India; re-elected leaders triple wealth', *Hindustan Times*, 15 June 2013

http://adrindia.org/media/adr-in-news/next-assembly-crorepatis, *The Times of India*, 24 October 2009

Chapter 6

'Protecting the highly protected', *The Economic Times*, 7 November 2013

'India is short of 0.5 million policemen but 47,000 protect VIPs', India Spend, 8 January 2013

Chapter 7

'LTA fraud: CBI files FIR against JDU MP Anil Sahani', IBNlive.com, 1 November 2013

'LTC scam: CBI seeks Rajya Sabha MP's fake travel bills', *The Times of India*, 5 November 2013

Chapter 8

'New dilemma for MPs: iPad or Galaxy?', *The Wall Street Journal*, 2 September 2011

'Indian MPs officially sanctioned iPads, but why?', www.nextbigwhat.com, 30 August 2011

'Manmonia's FSB: 3% of GDP', *The Financial Express*, 6 July 2013

Chapter 9

'Voters have a new option: reject all candidates', *Mint*, 27 September 2013

'Right to reject, will it matter?', *Tehelka*, 27 September 2013

'NOTA option does not mean right to reject and won't affect election results, says former election commissioner', *India Today*, 3 October 2013

'NOTA small matter, this', *The Hindu*, 9 October 2013

CHAPTER 10

'Evaluation Study on Total Sanitation Campaign, 2013', Planning Commission, Government of India, May 2013 http://planningcommission.nic.in/reports/peoreport/peo/rep_tscv1_2205.pdf

'India has more mobile phones than toilets: UN report', *The Telegraph*, 10 April 2010

'More mobile phones in India than toilets, says UN report', Press Trust of India, 16 April 2010

Key facts and figures on nutrition, UNICEF http://www.unicef.org/french/media/files/UNICEF_Key_facts_and_figures_on_Nutrition_Fr.pdf

'Forget Food Bill, India needs sanitation', *Wall Street Journal*, 10 July 2013

'Children in India, 2012, A Statistical Appraisal', Ministry of Statistics and Programme Implementation, 2012 http://mospi.nic.in/mospi_new/upload/Children_in_India_2012.pdf

The World Health Organisation http://www.who.int/mediacentre/factsheets/fs330/en/

'Clean hands, stay healthy,' *The Hindu*, 21 May 2012

'Only 53% wash hands after defecation', *The Times of India*, 6 July 2008

'The HUNGama Survey Report', Naandi Foundation, 2011 http://naandi.org/HungamaBKDecember11LR.pdf

CHAPTER 11

Report No. 3, 2010–11 http://www.cag.gov.in/html/reports/civil/ 2010-11_3PA/chap1.pdf

CHAPTER 12

'Bangla migration to India largest in developing world', *The Times of India*, 13 September 2013

'International migration report', United Nations Department of Economic and Social Affairs, 2013
http://esa.un.org/unmigration/wallchart2013.htm

'Demographic Invasion', *Outlook*, 13 August 2012

'South Asia Terrorism Portal: India Assessment 2013'
http://www.satp.org/satporgtp/countries/india/index.html

Chapter 13

'To empower dalits, do away with India's antiquated retail trading system', Chandra Bhan Prasad and Milind Kamble, *The Times of India*, 5 December 2012

'Rethinking Inequality: Dalits in Uttar Pradesh in the Markets Reform Era', Centre for Advanced Studies of India, University of Pennsylvania, *Economic and Political Weekly*, 28 August 2010

'Markets and Manu: Economic Reforms and its Impact of Caste in India, Centre for Advanced Studies of India', University of Pennsylvania, January 2008

Chapter 14

'People's Perception on Poverty Survey', CVoter, Whypoll Trust, United Nations Millennium Campaign, 2010
http://www.whypoll.org/images/Poverty_Final_Report.pdf

Chapter 15

'Shame: Delhi still India's rape capital', *The Times of India*, 4 June 2012

'We will not rape you like they did in the Delhi gang-rape case, but if you consent, we'll let you off', DainikBhaskar.com, 20 September 2013

'Gangrape controversy: Will burn my daughter alive if she had premarital sex, says defence lawyer', Zee News, 14 September 2013

'Taming Killer Buses', *Outlook*, 25 December 1996

Chapter 16

'Putting growth in its place', *Outlook*, 14 November 2011

'Delhi: teenager dies of dengue, 3,500 cases reported', PTI, 14 October 2013

'The fatal bite: dengue stings Delhi hard', *The Hindustan Times*, 5 November 2013

'India battles dengue fever outbreak', BBC.co.uk, 13 October 2013

Chapter 18

'Hafiz Saeed, My Story by Hafiz Saeed', *The Indian Express*, 8 April 2012

'Arundhati Roy, The Monster in the Mirror', *The Guardian*, 13 December 2008

Chapter 19

'The Fury of a Patient Man', *Fortune India*, July 2013

Chapter 20

'What is 2G scam all about?', *Reuters*, 27April 2011

'What is the Indian coal allocation scam?', *DNA*, 30 April 2013

'What the coal scam is all about', *The Hindu Business Line*, 20 August 2012

'The great Indian VVIP helicopter scam', Yahoo! News, 13 February 2013

'CAG blasts government in chopper scam: Auditor claims MoD set helicopter price higher than AgustaWestland itself requested', *The Daily Mail*, 14 August 2013.

'Performance Audit of Issue of Licences and Allocation of 2G Spectrum', Department of Telecommunications (Ministry of Communications and Information Technology), 10 November 2010

http://saiindia.gov.in/english/home/Our_Products/Audit_Report/Government_Wise/union_audit/recent_reports/union_performance/2010_2011/Civil_%20Performance_Audits/Report_no_19/Report_no_19.html

Report of the Comptroller and Auditor General of India on Acquisition of Helicopters from VVIPs, August 2013 http://saiindia.gov.in/english/home/Our_Products/ Audit_Report/Government_Wise/union_audit/recent_reports/union_compliance/2013/Defence/10of2013.pdf

'Performance Audit of Allocation of Coal Blocks and Augmentation of Coal Production (Ministry of Coal)', Comptroller and Auditor General of India, March 2012 http://saiindia.gov.in/english/home/Our_Products/Audit_Report/Government_Wise/union_audit/recent_reports/union_performance/2012_2013/Commercial/Report_No_7/Report_No_7.html

CWG scam: CVC recommends action against Suresh Kalmadi, FirstPost.com, 9 October2013

Report of the Comptroller and Auditor General of India on Performance Audit of XIXth Commonwealth Games 2010 http://saiindia.gov.in/english/home/Our_Products/Audit_report/Government_Wise/union_audit/recent_reports/union_performance/2011_2012/Civil_%20Performance_Audits/Report_No_6_CWG/Report_no_6_CWG.html

Chapter 21

'Debt do us part: India has to repay $172 billion debt by March 2014', *The Hindu*, 29 June 2013

'The ugly story of infrastructure, companies, banks, indiscriminate lending, and crippling bad debts', *Fortune India*, October 2013

'Minimum support price of wheat raised by Rs 50 to Rs 1400 a quintal', *The Times of India*, 18 October 2013

'Rajan won't raise India rate if prices soften, Adviser says', Bloomberg, 1 January 2014

Chapter 22

'PDS: A story of changing states', *Mint*, 7 August 2013

In Gujarat, the PDS is exclusionary and leaky, *The Hindu*, 19 August 2013

Chapter 23

'Communal Riots in India (A Chronology, 1947–2003)', Institute of Peace and Conflict Studies, March 2004

'Chronology of communal violence in India', Press Trust of India, 9 November 2011

'Hindu-Muslim Riots in India I & II, CERI', SciencesPo, Northwestern University, 20 August 2013
www.massviolence.org

Chapter 24

'Air pollution is a leading cause of cancer – UN agency', Reuters, 17 October 2013

'IARC: Outdoor air pollution a leading environmental cause of cancer deaths,' International Agency for Research on Cancer, 17 October 2013
http://www.iarc.fr/en/media-centre/iarcnews/pdf/pr221_E.pdf

'The carcinogenicity of outdoor air pollution', *Lancet*, 24 October 2013

'Beijing's bad air would be step up for smoggy Delhi', *The New York Times*, 25 January 2014

Chapter 25

'Excreta Does Matter', Centre for Science and Environment, May 2013

'Performance Audit of Water Pollution in India', Ministry of Environment and Forests, Comptroller and Auditor General of India, 2011–12

http://saiindia.gov.in/english/home/Public/In%20_Media/PR21_2011_12.pdf

Chapter 26

'Poison in India's groundwater posing national health crisis', *The Times of India*, 2 May 2012

http://www.worldbank.org/en/news/feature/2012/03/06/india-groundwater-critical-diminishing

Chapter 27

'Crimes against women up by 75 per cent in 15 years', *The Sunday Guardian*, 6 April 2013

Whypoll report, www.whypoll.org

Chapter 28

'Over 3 crore cases pending in courts in India: Govt', Press Trust of India, 7 May 2013

'India to have 15 crore pending cases by 2040, report says,' *The Times of India*, 17 January 2013

Chapter 29

'India placed 94th out of 176 countries in corruption: Transparency International', *The Hindu*, 5 December 2012
www.worldaudit.org/corruption

'Indian firms perform best in BRICS: corruption watchdog', *Reuters*, 17 October 2013

Chapter 30

'Farmers' suicide rates soar above the rest', *The Hindu*, 18 May 2013

'Farmer Suicides: The State's Killer Policies', *Forbes*, 7 November 2013

'International Farmer Suicide Crisis'
http://www.un.org/esa/sustdev/csd/csd16/PF/presentations/farmers_relief.pdf

Chapter 31

'Global Food Waste Not Want Not Report by the Institution of Mechanical Engineers',
http://www.imeche.org/docs/default-source/reports/Global_Food_Report.pdf

Chapter 32

'Global Hunger Index of the International Food Policy Research Institute' http://www.ifpri.org/publication/2013-global-hunger-index-0 2013

'India home to a quarter of the world's hungry: Global Hunger Index report', *The Times of India*, 15 October 2013

Chapter 33

'India's urban homeless increasing rapidly', *The Times of India*, 14 August 2013

'65 million people live in slums in India, says census data,' *The Hindu*, 1 October 2013

Chapter 34

'The Ailing Health of a Growing Nation, *The Wall Street Journal*, 30 July 2011

http://data.worldbank.org/indicator/SH.XPD.OOPC.ZS Out-of-pocket health expenditure (% of private expenditure on health)

'Rural India Faces 60% Shortage of Doctors', India Spend, 5 October 2012

'Heart disease cost India 9.2 mn productive years: PM', IANS, 1 March 2010

'Chronic diseases account for 53% of all deaths in India', *Mint*, 29 May 2007

'The Global Economic Burden of Non-Communicable Diseases', Harvard School of Public Health and the World Economic Forum, September 2011

http://www3. weforum.org/docs/WEF_Harvard_HE_GlobalEconomicBurdenNonCommunicableDiseases_2011.pdf

'India doesn't have even 1 hospital bed per 1,000 persons', *The Times of India*, 10 October 2011

Chapter 35

'Obesity on the rise in India, says Lancet', *The Indian Express*, 12 November 2010

'Global burden of obesity in 2005 and projections to 2030', *International Journal of Obesity*, July 2008

Chapter 36

'India's Fake Drugs Are A Real Problem', *Wall Street Journal*, 19 May 2010

http://www.ficci.com/sector/5/Add_docs/Knowledge%20Paper.pdf (FICCI report of fakes and counterfeit)

Chapter 37

'The state of the international organ trade: a provisional picture based on integration of available information', World Health Organisation, December 2007

Chapter 38

'India has just one operation theatre per one lakh people: Study', *The Times of India*, 4 July 2010

Chapter 39

UNICEF: Global, Regional and India Estimates http://www.unicef.org/india/hiv_aids.html

Department of AIDS Control, Ministry of Health and Family Welfare, 2011–12

http://www.aidsdatahub.org/sites/default/files/documents/NACO_Annual_Report_2011_12.pdf

Global Report (UNAIDS report on the global AIDS epidemic, 2013)

Chapter 40

'Indian State Finds Itself in Tight Grip of Addiction', *The New York Times*, 18 April 2012

'Drug abuse threatens Punjab's population', DW, 19 March 2013

'Moga is Punjab's drug capital', *The Times of India*, 8 June 2013

Chapter 41

'Liquor is the livelihood of India's Kerala state', *Los Angeles Times*, 11 July 2013

'Rum, rum everywhere', *The Economist*, 1 March 2013

Chapter 42

'India set to be heart disease capital of the world, say doctors', *The Indian Express*, 12 September 2012

'The Silent Killer', *Down to Earth*, 6 April 2013

World Health Organisation Fact Sheet: Bronchial Asthma http://www.who.int/mediacentre/factsheets/fs206/en/

World Asthma Day 2013: 10 facts about asthma you should know

http://health.india.com/diseases-conditions/world-asthma-day-2013-10-facts-about-asthma-you-should-know/

World Health Organisation: World TB Day 2013 http://www.searo.who.int/india/topics/tuberculosis/tbday_2013/en/index.html

'India Breast Cancer Surge Hinders Private Exams for Women', Bloomberg, 30 October 2013

World Health Organisation: Country Cooperation Strategy at a Glance http://www.who.int/countryfocus/cooperation_strategy/ccsbrief_ind_en.pdf

Chapter 43

Doing Business (The World Bank, International Finance Corporation) http://www.doingbusiness.org/rankings

The Global Competitiveness Index 2013-14 rankings http://www3.weforum.org/docs/GCR2013-14/GCR_Rankings_2013-14.pdf

2013 Index of Economic Freedom, The Heritage Foundation http://www.heritage.org/index/country/india

CHAPTER 44

'A bridge in Mumbai: Halfway to paradise', *The Economist*, 22 December 2012

'Mumbai local trains to get cosier', *The Hindustan Times*, 8 May 2010

'Mumbai building collapse fallout: 95 buildings declared dangerous to live in', http://ibnlive. in.com/news/mumbai-building-collapse-fallout-95-buildings-Decemberlared-dangerous-to-live-in/425370-3-237.html

'Mumbai: The 21st century city running on 19th century infrastructure', *The Economic Times*, 19 March 2013

'Mumbai: Milind Deora seeks Sonia Gandhi's help in Campa Cola demolition issue', Press Trust of India, 10 November 2013

CHAPTER 45

'Sewage plan raises a stink', *The Times of India*, 3 April 2013

Housing stock, amenities and assets in slums – Census 2011

'CAG report reveals only partial truth about sewage discharged into Yamuna', *Down To Earth*, http://www.downtoearth.org.in/content/cag-report-reveals-only-partial-truth-about-sewage-discharged-yamuna

'Performance audit of sewage management in Delhi', Comptroller and Auditor General of India, http://saiindia.gov.in/english../home/Our_Products/Audit_Report/Government_Wise/state_audit/recent_reports/Delhi/2012/Report_2/Chap_2.pdf

'Half of Delhi's population lives in slums', *The Times of India*, 4 October2012

'Seven-and-a-Half Million Cars Trigger Parking Wars in Delhi', *The New York Times*, 1 July 2013

Centre for Science of Environment

http://www.cseindia.org/userfiles/Parda%20Phash-27Septembert-1-CSE-Air.pdf

'Data on police organisations in India, as of 1 January 2012', Bureau of Police Research and Development http://bprd.nic.in/showfile.asp?lid=1047

'Delhi CM writes to Ambani over power dues', *The Hindu*, 4 June 2013

'Twenty two states fail to meet their Renewable Purchase Obligation: Delhi one of the worst performers', Greenpeace, 23 April 2013

http://webcache.googleusercontent.com/search?q=cache:http://www.greenpeace.org/india/en/news/Feature-Stories/Greenpeace-releases-renewable-energy-report-Delhi-produces-less-than-1/

'New solar power initiatives yielding results', *The Hindu*, 6 June 2013

Chapter 46

www.ined.fr

'World Population To Increase To 9.7B By 2050; India Will Overtake China As Most Populous Nation: New Study', *International Business Times*, 2 October 2013

'World population to reach 9.7 billion by 2050 new study predicts', AFP, 2 October 2013

Chapter 47

'Situation Analysis of the Elderly in India', The Ministry of Statistics and Programme Implementation, June, 2011,

http://mospi.nic.in/mospi_new/upload/elderly_in_india.pdf

'India's Frightening Secret: Many States Ageing More Than Scandinavia', India Spend, 2 July 2013

'The Second Transition: T. N. Ninan', *Business Standard*, 18 October 2013

Chapter 48

'Only 25 per cent of IT graduates readily employable: Nasscom', *The Economic Times*, 7 April 2011

www.pratham.org

'No lesson learnt, 50% Class 5 students can't read Class 2 books', *Pratham Books*,
http://www.pratham.org/NewsDetails.aspx?newsID=118
Employability and Skill Set of Newly Graduated Engineers, The World Bank, April 2011
http://elibrary.worldbank.org/doi/pdf/10.1596/1813-9450-5640
IDFC – India Infrastructure Report, 2012
http://www.idfc.com/pdf/report/IIR-2012.pdf
http://www.idfc.com/pdf/report/2012/Chapter_19.pdf
'A cut below', *Business* Today, 31 March 2013
'Where have all the jobs gone?, *The New Indian Express*, 25 August 2013
'Reaping India's promised demographic dividend', FICCI-Ernst & Young
http://www.ey.com/Publication/vwLUAssets/EY-Government-and-Public-Sector-Reaping-Indias-demographic-dividend/$FILE/EY-Reaping-Indias-promised-demographic-dividend-industry-in-driving-seat.pdf

Chapter 49

'Teacher absence in India, Harvard University', The World Bank, April-May 2005
http://www.teindia.nic.in/Files/Articles/Articles_23February12/jeea_teacher_absence_in_india.pdf
'India faces a shortage of 1.4 million trained teachers', *Deccan Chronicle*, 7 July 2013
'At 3 lakh, UP faces largest teacher shortage in India', *The Times of India*, 6 May 2013
'Para teachers in India: A Review, National Institute of Education Planning and Administration', UNESCO, October 2004
http://www.unesco.org/iiep/eng/research/basic/PDF/teachers5.pdf
Pratham, ASER, 2011
http://pratham.org/images/Aser-2011-report.pdf

'Teacher absenteeism on rise in UP: Report', *The Times of India*, 20 January 2011

'Reaching out of school children is crucial for development', UNESCO Institute for Statistics, June 2012 http://www.uis.unesco.org/Library/Documents/fs18-reaching-out-of-school-children-crucial-development-education-en.pdf

Chapter 50

The World Bank, Financial Inclusion Data

http://datatopics.worldbank.org/financialinclusion/

Speech on Financial Inclusion delivered by Dr. (Smt) Deepali Pant Joshi, Executive Director, Reserve Bank of India at the Vth Dun and Bradstreet Conclave on Financial Inclusion, Kolkata, 28 October 2013

http://www.rbi.org.in/scripts/BS_SpeechesView.aspx?Id=853

Chapter 51

'The World Economic Forum', *Global Gender Gap Index*, 2013,

http://reports.weforum.org/global-gender-gap-report-2013/

Chapter 52

'The World Economic Forum', *Global Risks Report*, 2013

http://reports.weforum.org/global-risks-2013/

Chapter 53

'The poor pay bribes of over Rs 8,000 million to access public services', August 2008, www.infochangeindia.org

www.cmsindia.org

Chapter 54

'India's Energy Policy and Electricity Production', National Bureau of Asian Research, 26 October 2011

'Power sector at a glance: All India', Ministry of Power http://www.powermin.nic.in/JSP_SERVLETS/internal.jsp

'India to build world's largest solar power plant in Rajasthan', Press Trust of India, 20 September 2013

'Tamil Nadu takes India's solar power capacity up 30%', *The Times of India*, 17 September 2013

'Over 1759 MW of projects commissioned under National Solar Mission', *The Times of India*, 27 July 2013

'2012: Power for All', Ministry of Power, http://www.powermin.nic.in/indian_electricity_scenario/power_for_all_target.htm

Chapter 55

'Manual scavenging: The worst job in India; PS: it's illegal too', *Mint*, 30 September 2013

'Manual scavengers: welfare and rehabilitation, August 2013'

http://164.100.47.134/intranet/Manual%20Scavengers%20welfare%20and%20Rehabilitation.pdf

'Delhi becomes the first state to ban manual scavenging', *The Hindustan Times*, 27 February 2013

Chapter 56 and Chapter 57

'Statistics show love is the most potent killer', *The Times of India*, 15 September 2013

'Crime in India 2012', National Crime Records Bureau

http://ncrb.gov.in/CD-CII2012/Compendium2012.pdf

Chapter 58

'India has 50 lakh child labourers', IANS, 11 June 2013

'Child Labour Drops 60% In A Decade But Still World's Highest', India Spend, 13 August 2013

Chapter 59

Ministry of Women and Child Development releases a study on Child Abuse, 9 April 2007

http://pib.nic.in/newsite/erelease.aspx?relid=26737

Chapter 60, Chapter 61 and Chapter 62

'Statistics show love is the most potent killer', *The Times of India*, 15 September 2013

'Crime in India 2012', National Crime Records Bureau

http://ncrb.gov.in/CD-CII2012/Compendium2012.pdf

'Student suicides soar 26 per cent in 5 years, education system blamed', *The Times of India*, 2 November 2011

Chapter 63

'India aiming to ease visa procedures to increase tourist arrivals: Chiranjeevi', *IANS*, 11 November 2013

UNWTO Tourism Highlights, 2013

http://dtxtq4w60xqpw.cloudfront.net/sites/all/files/pdf/unwto_highlights13_en_lr_0.pdf

'India tourist visits down 25% following fatal Delhi gang rape', *The Guardian*, 31 March 2013

Chapter 64

'India 121st in global information and communication technology rankings', *The Hindu*, 8 October 2013

Chapter 65

'India is now world's third largest Internet user after U.S., China', *The Hindu*, 24 August 2013

The Indian Telecom Services Performance Indicators, January–March, 2013

http://www.trai.gov.in/WriteReadData/WhatsNew/Documents/Indicator%20Reports%20-01082013.pdf

'Akamai: The State of the Internet Report, Second Quarter, 2013' http://www.akamai.com/stateoftheinternet/

Chapter 66

World Economic Forum: Global Information Technology Report 2013 http://www.weforum.org/reports/global-information-technology-report-2013

Chapter 67

World Economic Forum: The Human Capital Report, 2013 http://www3.weforum.org/docs/WEF_HumanCapitalReport_2013.pdf

Chapter 68

The Global Innovationation Index 2013 http://www.globalinnovationindex.org/content.aspx?page=gii-full-report-2013# pdfopener

Chapter 69

World Intellectual Property Indicators 2012 http://www.wipo.int/export/sites/www/freepublications/en/intproperty/941/wipo_pub_941_2012.pdf

'PM Manmohan Singh expresses concern over India's research output', *IANS*, 7 November 2013

'India sees sharp drop in patent application', *The Financial Express*, 8 January 2014

Chapter 70

'G20 countries, the worst and best for women' , TrustLaw, *Thompson Reuters*,
http://www.trust.org/spotlight/g20-countries-the-worst-and-best-for-women

http://www.trust.org/item/20120613010100-b7scy/?source=spotlight, 13 June 2012

Chapter 71

'India's bureaucracy 'worst in Asia'', BBC, 12 January 2012

Chapter 72

Global Peace Index, 2013
http://www.visionofhumanity.org/sites/default/files/2013_Global_Peace_Index_Report_0.pdf

Chapter 73

'World's worst airports to sleep in … and the best', Simon Busch, CNN, 22 October 2013
www.sleepinginairports.net

Chapter 74

JADEC Airline Safety Ranking 2012
http://www.jacDecember.de/jacDecember_safety_ranking_2012.htm

'Air India ranked world's third airline', *DNA*, 25 January 2013

Chapter 75

Bloomberg Businessweek, 4 March 2009
http://images.businessweek.com/ss/09/03/0304_difficult_cities/4.htm,

Chapter 76

Global Competitiveness Report, World Economic Forum, 2013–14
http://www.weforum.org/issues/global-competitiveness

'People's trust in politicians at all-time low in India: WEF', *Business Standard*, 26 September 2013

Chapter 77

Honour Based Violence Awareness Network
http://hbv-awareness.com/

Chapter 78

Global Slavery Index 2013, Walk Free Foundation
http://www.globalslaveryindex.org/

Chapter 79

'Global AgeWatch Index 2013', *Help Age International* http://www.helpage.org/global-agewatch/reports/

Chapter 80

'How India's construction workers get gypped of their due', India Spend, 5 September 2013

The Building and Construction Workers Related Laws (Amendment Bill) 2013

http://www.prsindia.org/uploads/media/Construction%20workers/Construction%20workers%20related%20laws%20bill.pdf

Ministry of Labour

http://labour.nic.in/content/dglw/Schemes/BuildingConstructionWorkers.html

Chapter 81

'India frontrunner in resume fraud', *Business World*, 24 October 2013

'10% of all CVs have false details, IT firms bear the brunt', *The Times of India*, 17 February 2013

Chapter 82

'20% of your food is adulterated', *DNA*, 10 August 2013

Chapter 83

'Are we safe? Some 5,400 dangerous criminals live amongst us!', India Spend, 21 June 2013

National Crime Records Bureau, Crime in India, 2012 http:// ncrb.gov.in/CD-CII2012/Compendium2012.pdf

Chapter 84

www.gunpolicy.org

Chapter 85

International News Safety Institute
http://www.newssafety.org/casualties.php

Chapter 86

'The 10 Countries With Notoriously Bad Tourists', *Business Insider*, 18 May 2013

Chapter 87

Kroll 2013/14 Global Fraud Report
http://www.kroll.com/media/KRL_FraudReport2013-14_USLetterPRESS_REVISED_ 10182013.pdf

Chapter 88

'In India, Tax Evasion Is a National Sport', *Bloomberg Businessweek*, 28 July 2011

'India's tax-GDP ratio one of the lowest', *Business Standard*, 26 March 2013

'Raise More Taxes to Fund Inclusive Development', Centre for Budget and Governance Accountability, Oxfam
http://www.oxfamindia.org/sites/default/files/raise%20more%20taxes%20to%20fund%20inclusive%20development.pdf

Chapter 89

'Union Budget 2013: Crorepati MPs grin and bear proposal to tax super rich', *The Times of India*, 1 March 2013

'Budget 2013: Why those 42000 crorepatis don't love Chidu anymore', Arun George, 28 February 2013
http://www.firstpost.com/budget2013/budget-2013-why-those-42000-crorepatis-dont-love-chidu-anymore-643249.html?utm_source=ref_article

Chapter 90

'Gold smuggling surges with govt's import curbs', *Business Standard*, 28 October 2013

'Gold Smuggling to Climb in India on Tax Increase, Festivals', Bloomberg, 14 August 2013

'India's gold rush: its impact and sustainability', ASSOCHAM, 1March 2012

http://www.assocham.org/arb/general/Indias_Gold_Rush_Its_Impact_and_Sustainability.pdf

Chapter 91

'Indian money in Swiss banks dips to record low at Rs 9,000 crore', PTI, 20 June 2013

Black money: In 2011, Rs 4L crore went out, a 24% rise, *The Times of India, 13 December 2013*

The 2013 Legatum Prosperity Index http://www.prosperity.com/#!/asia

Chapter 92

www.globalretailtheftbarometer.com

'India tops retail theft study for fifth year in a row', *Mint*, 19 October 2012

http://www.livemint.com/Companies/LClT9mKYoGyXoZwhsSozAI/India-tops-retail-theft-study-for-fifth-year-in-a-row.html

Chapter 93

Ministry of External Affairs, www.mea.gov.in, ttp://www.mea.gov.in/indian-foreign-service.htm

'Poor score on diplomatic count: India has only 845 diplomats while US has around 20,000', *The Economic Times*, 22 October 2013

'Shashi Tharoor wants to bring in 'experts' as diplomats', *India Today*, 30 May 2012

Chapter 94

'India loses $5 bn bid for Kashagan oil field to China', PTI, 2 July2013

'Chinese firm foils ONGC Videsh's $5 billion Kazakh deal', *Business Today*, 3 July 2013

'India's energy race with China sparks $4 billion loan rush', *Mint*, 17 October 2013

'China corners cheap OVL, GAIL gas from Myanmar, India cut out of deal', *The Financial Express*, 25 August 2013

CHAPTER 95

www.globalfirepower.com

http://www.globalfirepower.com/countries-comparison.asp

CHAPTER 96

'India accuses Pakistan of fresh attacks on Kashmir border posts', *The Guardian*, Associated Press, 13 October 2013

'Kashmir: India says eight civilians injured in Pakistan firing', 25 October 2013

'Ceasefire violation: Pak troops target 50 locations along international border, one BSF jawan killed, six injured', NDTV, 23 October 2013

CHAPTER 97

Highlights of the CAG Performance Audit of MNREGA, 31 May 2013, http://www.accountabilityindia.in/accountabilityblog/2640-highlights-cag-performance-audit-mgnrega

CHAPTER 98 AND CHAPTER 99

A version of these essays was first written by the author in the Indian edition of the *Fortune* magazine in November 2010 and January 2013.

CHAPTER 100

'Should I urinate to fill up empty dams? Ajit Pawar says', *The Times of India*, 8 April 2013

Link to NDTV video of Pawar's comment, 7 April 2013,

http://www.ndtv.com/video/player/india-this-week/ajit-pawar-s-shocking-remark-if-no-water-in-dam-do-we-urinate-in-it/270743

'Abhjit Mukherjee says Delhi gangrape protesters 'dented-painted' women, President asks him to apologise', PTI, 28 December 2012

'Majority of rapes in the state are consensual', *Mid Day*, 13 October 2012

YouTube link to the CNN-IBN show with Mamata Banerjee calling a college student Maoist,18 May 2012 http://www.youtube.com/watch?v=vx-2SsI4B9U

'Sorry Ma'am, but I am not a Maoist - Open letter to chief minister', *The Telegraph*, 20 May 2012

Link to NDTV video of Sharad Yadav's comment, 19 March 2013 http://www.ndtv.com/video/player/news/who-amongst-us-have-not-followed-girls-sharad-yadav-s-shocker/268979

'Won't apologise, says Abu Azmi, women must be escorted by male relatives', NDTV, 9 January 2013

'Chhattisgarh minister blames women's "stars" for crimes against them', PTI, 8 January 2013

'The Tripura model: growth marries development', *Governance Now*, 9 August 2013

'Unemployment level in State 9.9 percent', *The New Indian Express*, '15 March 2013

http://newindianexpress.com/states/kerala/article1502030.ece

'Sikkim has maximum unemployed; Chhattisgarh lowest: Report', PTI, 19 September 2013

Acknowledgements

I owe gratitude to the following:

D.N. Mukerjea, a sublimely refined, and genteel-ly critical boss, for saying, 'But of course you must write about politics. We are Bengalis.'

Brinda Vasudevan, encouraging friend and colleague, who said: 'After all, you do know that Tam Brahms and Bengalis basically bond on politics.'

Urvashi Suraiya, who said, 'Why don't you write a book so that I can understand some politics?' and later, gave terrific design feedback.

Shweta Punj, who said, 'We are not political at all, no, no, we merely discuss politics.'

Ishira Mehta and Simran Singh, who said, 'Authors need good friends to tell them all the time that they are wrong.'

Priya Doraswamy, the ever effervescent agent.

V. K. Karthika, ever zen (and always under pressure) publisher and editor.

Shantanu Ray Chaudhuri, eagle-eyed editor.

Ramona Sen, sharp, cutting and efficient copy editor, who read the book and said, 'Man, these MPs have a good life!'

Shuka Jain, the queen of last minute covers.

I thank India's unique, magnificent body polity and democratic traditions that never fail to astound or amuse.